EVERY DAY

AGENT

*Straight Talk & Proven
Methods to Grow Your
Real Estate Business*

WHITNEY ELLIS

What people are saying about *Every Day Agent*:

"In this book, Whitney Ellis has codified decades of proven strategies that ensure a real estate agent's success. The book is a 360-degree view of what it takes – boots on the ground – for an everyday agent to succeed. Attitude, foresight, tenacity, vision, entrepreneurial spirit, connections and pesistence. This book looks at every aspect of what a real estate career requires.

Every manager should have copies of this tactical handbook on hand to give to new agents who enter their offices. Every manager should consider giving this book to agents in their office who are struggling to help them get back on track.

This book is a how-to guide to get your career off to a solid start. Whitney has captured all the necessary elements, both soft skills and tactical strategies, that are required to succeed in today's challenging real estate market. Two thumbs up."

- Chris Leader, President and Master Trainer
Leader's Edge Training

"I found *Every Day Agent* to be a great resource for agents of all skill levels. A quick but thorough read. *Every Day Agent* is a well-thought-out, easy-to-follow guide. If implemented, this resource should be a great foundation to build a successful business."

- Cindi Rodgers, Managing Broker in Florida

"If you want to sell and list a lot of properties – if that is your goal – this book assists those wanting to sell themselves. *Every Day Agent* stresses: how crucial databases are, how to put yourself out there in the community, constant communication with sellers and buyers, and checklists that can actually prevent delayed closings. Whitney stresses the most accurate and important topics far more in-depth than the information in license classes!"

- Sandy Merritt, Agent in Florida for 19 years

"*Every Day Agent* has become my training manual for my team. Not only does it complement my own suggestions to achieve real estate success, but it articulates advice in a way I've personally never seen in print. It has been a great "refresher" for me to take my business to the next level!"

- Michael Orland, Director of Estate Properties in California

"*Every Day Agent* gave me a fresh perspective and new practices, as well as reminded me of daily habits that helped me find success earlier in my career. This book was informative and friendly at the same time. I felt like Whitney was cheering me on toward success!"

- Lora Carpenter, Corporate Relocation and Special Needs Relocation Realtor in Florida

ISBN-13: 978-0-578-57729-6

Cover Design: Tim Gilbert, Murton Way
Interior Design: Brianna Davis, Meraki Design
Editing: Cortni Merritt, SRD Editing Services

Printed in the USA

The information presented herein represents the view of the author as of the date of the publication. This book is presented for informational purposes only. Due to the rate at which conditions change, the author reserves the right to alter and update his opinions based on new conditions. While every attempt has been made to verify the information in this book, neither the author nor her affiliates/partners assume any responsibility for errors, inaccuracies, or omissions.

Table of Contents

EVERY DAY AGENT

Introduction: Why Did I Write Every Day Agent?

I had been a managing broker for more than five years, and teaching was my favorite part of the job. I loved seeing agents apply something they learned and enjoy a successful outcome. One day, I told my husband that I had met with an agent who I thought was going to be really great. He asked: "What makes a great agent?"

My answer came quickly and easily: *"The ones who work at it every day."*

Through my 15 years in the real estate industry, I have concluded that there is one reliable truth. In order to build a successful real estate career that is sustainable for years – even decades – you must work at it *every* day.

Now, I feel compelled to help others who face the same challenges I did as a beginning agent. Over the years, I went from being a top agent in my first three years, to new home sales, to managing a successful office. The knowledge and experience I gained is culminating in this book, which I plan as the first in my series that explores *proven methods to grow your real estate business and achieve success, every day.*

Every Day Agent is the book I wish I had when I was just starting out so I have created it for you in the hopes it will ease some of the uncertainty, fear and lack of direction that occurs while you are learning how to navigate this business.

Life-Changing Events Begin as Everyday Decisions

Mom, caregiver, community organizer & volunteer ready for more

What brought me into the real estate business? Well, it was a long road.

Growing up in Los Angeles, I was a latch-key child, the youngest of four to a single mother. We were happy and content, but never had two extra nickels to rub together. My mother showed me how to work hard and dream big; she made a good home for us with what she had. I started my first summer job when I was 13, working alongside my mother, which gave me experience in an office. I tried to manage college on my own, and attended a semester at Cal State Northridge, but lack of resources caused me to quit school and work full time in secretarial-type positions.

At the young age of 23, I was married with two children, and we moved from California to Florida. The financial struggles continued while I focused on being a mom, community organizer and volunteer. For so many years, I lived with the bare minimum. I wanted a better life.

Everyday decisions build on one another

When I was in my mid-30s, during a visit with my mother, she brought up the idea of getting my real estate license. Because I knew I needed to do something to make a better life for myself and my children, it made sense. I scraped together the money to take the licensing class, studied my heart out on nights and weekends and passed with high marks on my first try.

After I passed the exam, I made another "everyday decision." I had been working in the front office of my kids' high school at the time, and I chose to quit my job to dedicate myself to real estate. I joined a major brand name real estate company and took a leap of faith. What began as an everyday decision ended up being a new path to happiness, growth and success in my life.

A lot of drive but little direction

I took to my new career like a fish in water. The problem was: I had NO idea how to *sell* real estate. My brokerage boasted the best training, so I had hopes that I would get some guidance as to what to do in the *real* world of real estate. I attended every class and applied what I learned. I absorbed every word, took copious notes and really believed I could take the great information and turn it into a thriving real estate career!

I had a healthy "sphere of influence." I had lived in a tight community for more than a decade. I worked in pre-schools and daycares and volunteered for local elementary schools. I was PTO President for four years, set records with fundraising efforts, and did some substitute teaching to make ends meet.

I figured there would be *gold* in all my social relationships, since my sphere of influence was substantial. Surely, everyone who knew me would want me to handle their next real estate transaction! I wrote letters, sent cards and told everyone about my new career, patiently waiting for the phone to start ringing with new opportunities. But ... I think you know where this is headed.

The payoff of dedication

Fast forward about two months, during which time I joined the local Realtor association and took classes to learn the MLS system and how to "play nice in the sandbox" with other agents. But even after all this, I felt lost.

Eventually, a floor time shift at the office paid off; I had my first buyer prospect. I distinctly remember the terror that overtook me the moment the couple said, "Yes! We would like to make an offer on this house!"

I know what you're thinking – I should have been thrilled! elated! ecstatic! But I remember nothing except the feeling of panic, because I just *knew* that I was not prepared to help these people buy a home.

In the end, we made it through a successful purchase, then they used me to list the house they already owned. As my career began to pick up, I realized that the panic was normal and could aid me, if I learned to utilize it. I learned that working efficiently and with kindness and gratitude would always leave me, my clients and my fellow agents feeling positive after a transaction. And I began to learn the "tricks of the trade" that would benefit me for years to come.

It wasn't easy, but as I applied the lessons I was learning, I started to see results. In my first few years, I earned company awards and was operating in the top 10% of my office.

From agent to managing broker

As years went by, my business grew and became stronger. A move from the Space Coast to the Gulf Coast of Florida had me again facing new challenges, during the great recession. Being in an unfamiliar area, I had to position myself in a place where I could succeed without knowing the area or having an established sphere of influence. I was able to secure a position selling high-end, waterfront condos without any previous experience in that type of sale, then shifted from condo sales to new home sales. Within only a few years, I was consistently recognized as a top producer in my office and was asked to join the Leadership Development Program.

I obtained my broker's license and was offered a position as managing broker. I soon discovered that this was the position that I was made for – coaching agents to success! I recruited, retained and grew profitability, crafting the office culture to one of collaboration and productivity, with a high emphasis on performance coaching.

I've always loved helping people, and I am grateful for the privilege to enjoy doing that every day.

Bringing My Message to You: The Mission of *Every Day Agent*

I have written *Every Day Agent* to help people who are starting out in the business, stuck in a rut, or looking to take their business to the next level. I take great joy in helping other people who are struggling to find their true potential and the ultimate realization of their dreams.

The book is organized into four parts to help you:
1. Set yourself up for success.
2. Increase your productivity.
3. Dig into the "meat and potatoes" of what makes an agent great.
4. Become your clients' realtor for life.

Through these pages, I hope you enjoy the strategies, tips and techniques that I've shared. When applied daily, these easy-to-follow processes lead to long-term results. If you apply these proven strategies to your business and you take deliberate action, you will find success beyond your wildest dreams. You can be the agent you dream of being, while helping people and growing your financial wealth at the same time!

A Choice for Change

In life there is a path
Which leads to the treasures we seek
Settled into the comforts of our own reality
Blessings not recognized until they are gone

Eyes cast downward not wanting to see
Ignored by our own ignorance; the writing on the wall escapes our glance
Moved by another what was meant to be ours
Stripping our world of our entitlement
What we know is gone, leaving only a paralyzing fear
A choice to be made

To lock away in darkness never seeking more
Believing in nothing but what has been taken away
Or, alas to break through the binding fear
Dare to face the unknown corridors to see the hope of a new reality
Each step a journey, opening pathways
Shining new light

Fear cast aside, crashing through the roadblock which lies within
To find a new beginning better than before
The treasure we seek ever changing, always moving
The courage to never stop wondering
Discovering that which brings joy unimagined

~ Whitney Ellis
March 19, 2011

11

EVERY DAY AGENT

PART ONE – SET YOURSELF UP FOR SUCCESS

Chapter One: Reality Check – Is Real Estate Right for You?

A big part of making the decision to begin a real estate career is understanding the REALITY behind this industry. So many people think that real estate is fun, easy and glamorous! They have visions of pulling up to a beautiful house in their luxury car, with a well-qualified couple, and opening the door to the home of their dreams. Sounds ideal, doesn't it? Well, I have news for you – what you see on HGTV is *not* a true "day in the life" of a real estate agent. Shocked?

While real estate varies greatly from market to market and state to state, there are a few universal truths to consider. For one, real estate is a *full-time* job and not as flexible as you might believe. In the beginning, you will put in a lot of time without immediate reward. Sure, you might get lucky and have a ready, willing and able buyer walk into your first open house – but don't count on it!

The first few months in the business, you will (and should) spend your time learning. Hopefully, the company or brokerage you joined has a training or mentoring program to help you get started. If they don't, you need to develop your own plan to gain the skill and knowledge needed to begin working with customers. Take classes available at your local association to learn the programs you'll use, including the Multi-Listing Service (MLS) system. Once you achieve a level of comfort with these things, you can begin to host open houses for other agents in your office and get on the schedule for "floor-time" or "up-time," if that is available at your office.

Set up profiles and start generating content on your website, social media and other online forums. You need to begin building a database – Gathering the names, phone numbers and email addresses of *everyone* you have ever known and adding them to your Customer Relationship Management (CRM) system.

Then, when one strategy pays off, and you finally show a house, don't be surprised when something goes wrong. The key could be missing from the lock box, you might accidentally let the cat out, the place could have a pungent odor or look like it is occupied by a family of goats.

Showings are not always glamorous. Real estate agents often run into situations that require quick thinking. More than once, I have scheduled a showing, knocked loudly on arrival – then entered to find the occupant asleep in bed or getting out of the shower! I have been chased by alpacas and barked at by vicious dogs. You will show vacant houses that feel like the floors (or roof) may cave, or that smell like mold (or worse). You get the picture.

The good news is: The next day, you could be showing a multi-million-dollar beachfront oasis. You never know!

Don't fret. As hard as it can be, many people find great satisfaction and success in real estate. As much as it has its challenges, it can also be very rewarding. Having realistic expectations is key to long-term success. This field is not for everyone. Many people fail, because they didn't prepare with the right information.

So, how do you make sure real estate is right for you? Or that *you* are right for real estate? Ask yourself, with brutal honesty, if you can fully commit. Consider the following:

One: Are you willing and able to work in real estate full time?

Most people are *willing* to put in the work and time. They begin a real estate venture with the best intentions. But are you also able to do what it takes? Another job, either full- or part-time, doesn't make it impossible to start a real estate career, but it can cause scheduling conflicts. You may think real estate is "flexible," but, the truth is, if you aren't available when a client calls, you will likely miss that opportunity.

Working real estate around raising a family has its own challenges. Daycare and school schedules complicate your week, family activities complicate your week-ends; maybe your spouse helps out, but this too can create obstacles to opportunities. Unless you have a solid support system for your childcare needs, even when the tots are sick, these conflicts can be a showstopper.

Two: Do you have the ability to work for 4-6 months, without an income?

Dividing time between your real estate career and another job may stack the odds against you, compared to agents who can dedicate all their time and effort to their real estate careers. If you're in this position, you should plan to give yourself a financial cushion. Have a nest egg set aside to cover living expenses; it frees you up to focus on your business.

In addition, you must *invest* in your business. The adage remains true: *You have to spend money to make money*. There are many free and low-cost resources shared with you throughout this book. But you *will* have to initially lay out funds before you get your first commission check. Be prepared.

Three: Do you have the drive and motivation to get through the tough stuff?

If you think real estate is fun and easy, then I challenge you to take a long, hard look at your decision to go down this path. If you see real estate as a business where you can be your own boss, and you are willing to work at it *every day*, you might just be successful. In this business, you must work; you must apply your unique ideas and talents, while helping people buy and sell homes. Your drive and motivation are key factors in navigating the difficult aspects of your real estate business. Are you willing to dig deep? Nobody likes making tough commitments, but if you lock in your commitment to work hard and overcome obstacles, your dedication will be rewarded!

Locking in the Commitment

In order to succeed, you must get up every day and go to *work*. Put on your real estate costume and get out there. You will need to push beyond your comfort zone. You will feel lost. You will get disappointed. Just know that it *all* leads to growth.

So, how do you keep going? First, having realistic expectations is key. It's easier to roll with the punches when you know they will come. Dealing with disappointment is a reality, and you need to grow a thick skin. It's business, not personal. Sometimes that is hard to separate, which can become paralyzing. Keep your eye on the prize. Know there is plenty of reward at the end of your effort.

You will need to set realistic timelines to track your progress and reinforce your commitment on a regular basis. As you set and achieve milestones, your confidence and commitment will grow. Make daily, weekly and monthly goals that move your business forward and remember to keep your focus on income-generating activities.

Every Day Action Item:

> Identify an accountability partner to help keep you honest. This can be a coworker, family member or your manager or broker. Commit to following the steps in this book and working at your business every day.

Your commitment to income-producing daily activities is a great first start to long-term success in real estate.

Now that you have made the commitment, let's figure out your *"Why"* and set some goals.

Chapter Two: Find Your Motivation – What Lights Your Fire?

As you navigate through your real estate career, you will be asked to step outside your comfort zone. You will need to practice discipline and push yourself to work without a boss to answer to.

So, what will keep you going? What is your "*Why*"?

Having a clear definition of *why* you do what you do is a key factor in success. If you started a real estate career merely to "fill time during retirement," if you don't really *need* the money, what might happen when you are told that the best way to get listings is by knocking on doors in a specific neighborhood or calling "For Sale by Owner" listings? These are not easy or fun tasks, and if you don't *have* to, you probably won't.

Money Isn't Everything

Don't get me wrong, your motivation does not have to be money. Let's take the same example but add one factor: You are the type of person who craves *achievement* or is driven by *recognition*.

If this desire is strong enough, it will get you through tough spots. You may have a desire to help people. Some very successful agents start their career because of a bad real estate experience! Those agents were passionate about being professionals who conduct themselves a certain way, and who maintain a high level of knowledge and standards. They got into the business to do it better – and the reward they received was the satisfaction of a job well done.

These are all great motivators but to be honest – for many, the most compelling motivator is the almighty dollar. For some people, money is a "want," but for most people, it is a *need*.

Which sounds more like you?:

> "*I have enough money now to live comfortably, but I would like to travel more or buy a new car or a bigger house.*"

Or

> "*I need to make money to provide for myself and my family. We need shelter, food, healthcare and clothing – as well as saving for our future.*"

In either case, the more you define your *Why*, the more it helps you muster the discipline needed to succeed in real estate.

In the next chapter you will be asked to identify your specific goals. You may say you want to make $100,000 next year, and that's a great goal! But I want you to think first about *why* you want $100,000 – what will that money mean to you? Is it saving for your kids' education, travel, or buying a big house or a "dream" car?

Your *Why* should light a fire in your belly when you think about it. You should feel hope, excitement, anticipation. Picture your daughter opening her acceptance letter to Harvard and imagine the feeling of pure satisfaction, knowing that you can help her make that dream a reality. Think about that epic vacation you want to take with your family each summer – without any worry about the expense.

Envision yourself relaxing in that dream house or driving that car and **get excited!**

I would be remiss to talk about your *Why* without also talking about passion. While not necessarily the same thing, these two pieces of the puzzle are closely related. Consider this quote:

> *"You can only become truly accomplished at something you love. Don't make money your goal. Instead pursue the things you love doing, and then do them so well that people can't take their eyes off of you." – Maya Angelou*

Starting a new business comes with growing pains, and it takes time to reap financial rewards. But if you are truly passionate about what you do, and you know **why** you are doing it, there are no obstacles that cannot be overcome.

Every Day Action Item:

Take out a sheet of paper and write down everything that comes to mind pertaining to why you want to sell real estate – just let everything flow out of you until you fill the page. Now, identify the one thing – the thing that lights a fire in your belly. This is your Why. I recommend you place a visual reminder somewhere you can see it.

Trust me, you will need this reminder as you push yourself outside your comfort zone.

Chapter Three: Set Goals – Find Your True North

There are endless schools of thought on goal setting – and many are effective. The important thing is to find one that feels right to you and do it. I am a firm believer in written goals and visualization, but there is no one right (or wrong) way to set your goals.

However you do it, having a clear end in mind is crucial. You would never start a long trip without first looking at a map and charting a course, would you? It's difficult to get somewhere if you don't know where you're going.

Think of your goals as your GPS. You plug in where you want to end and set the turn-by-turn directions to get there. Along the way, have recognizable milestones to keep yourself going in the right direction. This way, if you are off track, you can make course corrections before you get completely lost!

Real Estate Career Goals

When it comes to specific real estate goals and business planning, follow three universal guidelines:

Break it down

If you say, "I want to make $100,000 this year," that's great, you have a goal in mind. But in order to be effective, you need to break it down into smaller pieces, or steps, that can be visualized and followed.

For Example:

At an average price point of $200,000, I would need to do 24 transactions (two closings per month). This would result in $144,000 annual gross income. Subtract brokerage fees and/or split and marketing costs, which results in about $100,000 annual income. Now, you have a clear path to follow. If you are not closing two deals per month, then you know to make course corrections, or you will not end up where you want to be at the end of the year.

Breaking down your goals helps them feel more attainable. If you kept it at 24 transactions, that might be overwhelming. If it doesn't feel realistic or achievable, you are less likely to take action. But when you break it down to two transactions per month, then it feels like something you can manage!

Make it visual

Put the numbers related to your goals in a place where you will see them every day. Put a visual reminder of your goal on your mirror, car steering wheel, computer screen – wherever you look several times every day! You want to see it every day. Ask yourself: "Am I on track to close two transactions this month? What do I need to do today to ensure I reach that number?"

We will break this down in our business planning section below, so stay tuned.

Maybe you are wired differently, and your goals are recognition based. You might say, "I want to accept the *Silver Elite* award at the company awards ceremony my first year."

If *that* is what puts the fire in your belly, then by all means – write *Silver Elite* in big, bold letters where you can see it every day. Then, write what you need to do to get there. If the criteria for the *Silver Elite* award is $3 million in production volume, then, using the same example from earlier, you will need to do 15 transactions at an average price point of $200,000, to reach that goal. **Make. It. Visual.**

Create a Big Hairy Audacious Goal – a BHAG

Dig deep and set a Big Hair Audacious Goal – a BHAG! (It's pronounced "Bee-hag.") For more on how to set your own BHAGs, check out the book by Jim Collins and Jerry I. Porras, *Built to Last: Successful Habits of Visionary Companies.*

The experts tell you that your goals should be "attainable" – I challenge you to swing for the fences on this one. Be realistic, but don't limit yourself. If you think you can easily do two transactions each month, why not put in a little more effort and aim for four? The only thing stopping you, is *you.* Let's put these methods to the test and see where they take you.

Adjust your attitude

Are you an Eeyore? Or are you a Tigger?
I have had newly licensed agents, interested in joining my office, who say, "I know it takes a long time to get started in this business, and it will probably take a year to get my first sale." Well, with that mindset, they are probably right!

I have had others who look up at our production board and say, "I am going to put my name on that board next month," or "I want to be one of your top 10 agents in two years!"

Not only can they achieve this, but people around them will be inspired to help them when they have the right attitude! To achieve, you must first believe. Then, take appropriate *action*.

Every Day Action Item:

Break down your numbers. Put your goals somewhere that you can see them *frequently*. Setting realistic goals is one thing, but you also need to consistently align your daily activities with your ultimate goals. Put a daily reminder in your calendar and ask yourself often if your activities are getting you closer to your goals.

Chapter Four: Business Plans – Be Deliberate

Now that you have a clear goal, you need to set the pathway to get there. Setting your goals is great, but now you need to apply specific daily activities. You need a *plan*.

Have you ever heard the saying, "A goal without a plan is just a dream?" The tools and concepts in this book are going to show you daily habits and activities that will get you to your goals!

Every Day Agent Resource: Business Plan

For your Business Planning Guide, visit the resource section at EverydayREAgent.com.

The important thing is that you break your plan down and *put it in writing*. In this guide, you will identify the specific activities you should be doing every day and schedule those activities into your daily and weekly calendar.

Rules of a Real Estate Business Plan

Some realities about real estate business planning:
- If it's not easy, you won't follow it – so keep it simple.
- This is not a job, it's a business – commit to work at it every day.
- There will be obstacles, and you need to know how to overcome them.
- You will have to step outside your comfort zone – keep your "Why" in mind.

Using the same example we used in the Chapter Three section "Break it down", let's say you want to make $100,000 this year, and the average price point in your market is $200,000. On average, about one out of three appointments results in a closed transaction, and it takes an average of 10 contacts to get an appointment.

Using these averages, consider the following example to break down your daily activities. Remember, you will need to adjust your numbers based on your individual goal and market.

For Example:

Income Goal Divided by average commission per transaction	$100,000 4,100
Number of transactions (It takes 3 appointments to = 1 closing)	24
Number of appointments required (It takes 10 contacts to get 1 appointment)	72
Number of contacts required per year Divided by number of workdays (5 days x 50 weeks)	720 250
Contacts required per workday (rounded)	3

You need to close 24 transactions during the year to reach your goal. So, how do you put the plan in place to ensure you close 24 transactions? In order to achieve this, you need to make three (3) quality contacts, five (5) days every week.

Pro Tip:

> As you begin to close transactions, it is essential that you put a system in place to track where your business comes from. Start a simple spreadsheet at the beginning of the year, showing the client name, property address, transaction side, purchase price and lead source. This is not your CRM, it is a business tracker, so you can see which efforts are paying off, giving you the information that you need to fine-tune your future marketing and lead-generation efforts.

Quality Contacts

In addition to focusing on the number of contacts you make every day, I challenge you to take a good look at the quality of those contacts. Many people will try to sell you leads. You do **not** need to buy leads to become successful.

The key is to talk to people who know and like you, and those who have a real estate need. Sounds simple, right? Well, it is!

Stop concentrating on cold calls and random neighborhood door knocking. Don't get me wrong, you **will** need to call people, and you **will** need to knock on doors! But, if you do it with a purpose, you will get results.

People don't want to be cold called, and for the most part, don't even have landlines anymore. They are so inundated with solicitation calls, they generally don't answer the phone if they don't recognize the number, and if they do, are quick to hang up as soon as they hear your opening pitch. Door knocking has challenges as well. Non-solicitation rules, gated neighborhoods or homes that are farther apart make the time spent less efficient and less effective. There is a better way!

We will delve more into this when we talk about *prospecting*. Right now, focus on building that pathway to reaching your goal – your business plan.

In order to get a better picture of your daily activities – first, let's define what a "contact" is.

Commenting on a Facebook post or sending someone a private message (also known as a direct message, PM, DM and other shorthand) is **not** a contact. A contact is a face-to-face or voice-to-voice interaction. I know you don't want to hear this, but it might be the most important message I have to convey to you in this book:

> *If you can get comfortable with face-to-face and voice-to-voice contact, you are on your way to a successful real estate career.*

It is too easy to hide behind passive activities such as social media, or to feel accomplished, because you left a couple of voicemails. Your inner voice might tell you: "Well, I tried, but no one answered. Guess I'll just call it a day!"

The same goes for social events. You might have joined a networking group or a club in order to be around more people, but if you aren't having meaningful conversations relating to real estate – then, you are just wasting your time. I am not saying that you should not be doing these things, you should, but there is a time and a place for passive lead generation.

The important thing is to do it deliberately as part of your plan. Know the difference between *passive* and *active prospecting*.

> ## CONTACT
> ### A face-to-face or voice-to-voice interaction.

So, what is our ultimate goal? The answer is **appointments**. Your daily focus should be on activities that are going to generate appointments.

You have broken down your specific goals and come up with the number of contacts you need every day. Using the example, you need to make three contacts per day, and you need to have about two appointments per week to result in your goal of two closings every month.

Be relentless. Don't let anything get in the way of your plan!

Every Day Action Item:

Identify your "goal number" and write down where you can see it every day. Once you have identified how many houses you need to sell in a year, put up a visual somewhere.

One agent I know put 12 little houses up on a board in her house. Every time she closed a transaction, she put an X through one of the houses. Great idea!

Do the same thing with appointments or even contacts. Put 20 business cards in your pocket at the beginning of the day, and don't go home until you have given them all out in a meaningful way!

Give yourself visual reminders of your goals and the daily actions needed to reach them.

What's Stopping You?

I could easily list 50 different activities that you could do to generate those appointments – but the idea is to keep it simple, right? As a new agent, I am going to help you focus in on the top five activities that you should be doing on a recurring basis to kick-start your business. You can do five things, right?

Of course, you can. The key is that you need to do them well, consistently, and deliberately.

Before we push on, we need to talk a little about the "F word." Because at this point, it's really the only thing that is going to get in the way. I want you to ask yourself:

> *If you have the five things that you need to be doing every day, what is going to stop you?*

Especially if I tell you that by doing these things consistently and with great skill, you WILL meet your goals.

The answer, whether you are willing to admit it or not, is the "F word" … **FEAR.**

Chapter Five: Fear – Kick It to The Curb

There will always be excuses. You wake up with the best intentions, you have your schedule set for the day, and this time, you swear nothing is going to derail your plans.

Then, life gets in the way. Your spouse asks you to drop off the dry cleaning, the kids need a ride somewhere, the dog needs a bath, the laundry is piling up – whatever it is. There is always something.

Reality Check: This Work is Scary

Think of this: If you had a 9 a.m.-5 p.m. job, with a boss and a time clock, you would find other ways to either handle or delegate these interruptions. So, why do you let them disrupt your carefully planned business?

Well, **number one**, because you can. And, **number two**, because it is an excuse to avoid the things you don't want to do.

Let's face it – many of the things you *must* do every day to build your real estate business are not fun. They are outside your comfort zone, and you don't want to do them.

This apprehension comes from fear. Fear of rejection, fear of failure, and sometimes, oddly enough, fear of success. Because of this underlying fear, you allow the other noise of the day to stop you from doing the things you know you need to do. You need to be stronger than the excuses!

What Did the Wizard of Oz Tell the Cowardly Lion?

Answer: **You had the courage within you all along.**

This is where your *Why* comes in. If you know *why* you are building a real estate business, you can draw on that whenever you feel yourself getting derailed from your plan. Take those moments to center yourself and remember why it's so important to reach that goal. This is where you need to find a way to get beyond this barricade. It's important to confront the feelings you have, acknowledge them, then push past them, and start knocking out those activities on your schedule.

Do It Anyway

If this is a big challenge for you, I highly recommend the book by Susan Jeffers, *Feel the Fear ... And Do It Anyway*. This book delves deeply into this subject and can help you change your thinking, and therefore, change your actions and reactions to fear.

In her book, she defines what she calls "Level Two Fears," such as:

Rejection	Success	Failure
Being Vulnerable	Helplessness	Disapproval

Do any of these sound familiar?

Keep in mind that fear is a primal impulse – it is there to protect you, and literally keep you alive. It takes a very strong conviction to overcome this deep-seated instinct. Being aware of this is the first step to getting past it. Then, you can start to reason through what exactly is causing the fear.

Attack your fear: Procrastination

Let's say, for example, your daily to-do list starts with working expired listings. You do the research on a couple of listings that expired yesterday and have the seller's phone number jotted down. It's 10 a.m., a perfectly reasonable time to make the phone call, but you say, "You know, I really should get that laundry started," or "I've got some emails to answer." These excuses have entered your head, because you don't want to make the phone call.

You are going to elect to do the easy things over the hard things – because of fear. But fear of what? What is the worst thing that could happen if you pick up the phone and call that seller? Are you going to die? Of course, the answer is no.

You have to tell yourself – *I am not going to die. Nothing is going to cause me harm by making this call. The worst thing that will happen is they will tell me "no."*

Attack your fear: Build your confidence

Another fear that could add to your hesitation is the fear that you don't know what to say, or that they might ask you a question that you don't know how to answer. You might be afraid that they might be angry or rude. They might hang up on you, or worse, they might say "No."

The best way to prevent this fear from stopping you is to be *prepared*. I am not a fan of scripts, per se. However, it is very important that you **have practiced talking points** to guide you through the conversation. If you aren't prepared to have the conversation, you won't make the call!

Have an opening line. The rest of the conversation is going to depend on the particular responses from the seller. Because your main objective is to get an appointment, you don't have to be prepared to answer all their questions and solve all their problems. You do, however, need to be prepared to get an appointment – so, practice your skills and have your talking points ready. I will be sharing some of these opening lines and talking points later in the book, so stay with me!

Attack your fear: Get comfortable hearing "No"

Feel confident about answering objections and asking for the appointment. Have your schedule in front of you, so you are ready to suggest your next couple of openings. And finally, it's not the end of the world if they say "no." Remember, it takes 10 contacts to get one appointment – so this "no" just got you closer to your next "yes"!

Think of this popular abbreviation: SW, SW, SW, Next!

It means:
> *Some Will. Some Won't. So What? Next!*

I recommend you print this in large font and hang it somewhere visible while you are making your calls!

Every "no" gets you one step closer to that "YES!" It's important to note that "no" often means "not now," so don't immediately give up on this person, just put them aside for later.

Another thing to keep in mind is that the best time to make a phone call is right after you got a "YES" – so just because you got the appointment, don't stop calling! Your confidence and energy will be at its best, so keep at it and go for another one!

Every Day Action Item:

When you find you are talking yourself out of doing something that makes you uncomfortable, stop and ask yourself, "What is the worst that could happen?"

Then consider: What is the best that could happen? Remember your Why and push past the fear.

PART TWO – PRODUCTIVITY

Chapter Six: Time Management – Activity Triage

I am going to be very realistic with you in this chapter – managing your time as a real estate agent is challenging. It takes a lot of discipline, something that can be difficult for most of us. As an independent business owner, you don't have a predetermined job description and well-defined daily tasks. You also don't have anyone to answer to but yourself.

Avoiding a "Feast or Famine" Pattern

New-to-the-business agents often become paralyzed, because they don't know WHAT they should be doing. Then, they become discouraged because the things they are doing aren't showing immediate results. The other pitfall you can fall into is that as soon as you start getting a little busy, you focus all your time and attention on that activity and stop doing the things that will build more business. You are working *in* your business instead of *on* your business. This is what causes the "feast or famine" syndrome – but it is preventable!

Realistic scheduling

If you have done any research or read any books on managing your real estate business, you have probably heard a lot of suggestions that you need to set a schedule or "time block" to ensure you get things done. You may have even bought fancy calendar programs or scheduling books, attempting to keep yourself "on task." Others may tell you that your day should look like:

6 a.m.	Get up early! Do affirmations, drink water, do some exercise, eat breakfast.
7 a.m.	Get ready for your day, dress for success.
8 a.m.	Answer emails, deal management, check your hot sheets.
9 a.m.	Two hours of solid calling!
11 a.m.	Check email and deal management.
Noon	Lunch with past client.
1-5 p.m.	Attend appointments.

I am not saying that these are not all worthy activities – they are! But take a close look at this timeline. Tell me, what's wrong with it? If you think it might be a little unrealistic, I would say you are right. If you set a schedule like this every day of the week, you are most likely setting yourself up to fail. Then you feel bad about failing to do what you were determined to do, and you just give up and go back to winging it.

Prep time is real time (Not "down time")

Why is the above example unrealistic? Because, when you are starting out, things usually take longer than you think. One of the things that always strikes me about these "suggested schedules" is that there is no travel time built in. There is also a significant lack of prep time built into this schedule.

If I am expected to do "two solid hours of calling", when was I supposed to work on my database to determine who I will call and define the purpose of my call? There are many things that come at you every day, and some of them could lead to immediate business – so, you must have time to handle the everyday minutia as it comes at you.

Balance + Prioritization = Productive Time Management

I believe the answer to successful time management is **balance**. If you find balance between a strict regimented schedule and things you must do on a regular basis to continue to grow your business, you will find *productivity*.

Every Day Agent Resource: Productive, Managed Calendar

How to build your calendar

I suggest keeping a "month at a glance" calendar (either physical or virtual), and fill in the time as follows:

One: Start with things that are not negotiable. Fill in the family activities that you want or need to attend: Parent night at school, field trips, volunteer days, date night with your significant other, family outings, etc. This category should also include scheduled closings!

Put those down in permanent ink and protect them from being bumped by business appointments. Remember to stay realistic – sometimes you must be flexible, and sometimes you do have to put business first. The important thing is to make sure it is *your* decision. You control your schedule; it does not control you.

If you are laser-focused on building an empire, and nothing is going to get in your way, then business appointments might take precedence over personal events. If family and social activities are very important to you, then those things should have priority – as long as you are doing the work you need to do to reach *your* desired goals. So, **you** determine the things that are non-negotiable and put those in your calendar first!

Two: Fill in office or professional events. Sales meetings, trainings, networking events that you would like to attend. These are going to be prioritized on a case-by-case basis. These types of activities are important to your business and personal growth; they should only be bumped by an appointment with a prospect who cannot possibly meet you at any other time. This is something I see happen every day.

Agents skip a meeting or appointment where they missed important information or valuable skill-building activities in favor of showing a house to a buyer. What I find when I probe them is that they didn't really try to protect that activity. They say that a buyer called and asked to go see a house, so they adjusted their day accordingly. What if the agent had said "I can't do 2 p.m., but I can do 3:30. Would that work?"

Nine times out of 10 the buyer will be fine with that. Are there ever exceptions? Of course! Perhaps the buyer is leaving town later that afternoon, and the time they suggest is the only possible opportunity to see the house. If this is a qualified, serious buyer, then you might opt to miss the event and show the house. Or, if you are in a hot market where the buyer might lose out on the house if you don't act fast, then you might have to make that choice. Is that extra hour really going to matter? If yes, then go show the house. The point is that it is a *decision*, not just a *reaction*.

Three: Schedule your Open Houses. For the most part, these are non-negotiable. However, if a drop-dead important alternative appointment comes up during the time you have scheduled an open house, you could consider having the open house covered by another agent in your office. Scheduled open house events should never be cancelled.

Four: Define your ideal appointment times. When you are making your appointments, it is okay to say, "I am available on Tuesday evening from 5-7 p.m. or Friday morning at 10 a.m. – which is better for you?" Start by suggesting the days and times that work best for you, but you will need to be flexible on this. Stay within the guidelines set forth in this chapter.

Remember your goals from Chapter Three. How many appointments do you need to have every week in order to stay on track? Make sure you block out enough time on your calendar to hold at least that many appointments – adding in a few alternate times for flexibility.

If you work with buyers, you will need to allow time for home tours. As you schedule time to show homes to buyers, be sure to allow enough time, taking into consideration how many homes they want to see and how large of a search area you are covering. You may spend an entire day with a buyer, or you may have someone who has one or two specific homes they want to see. Plan accordingly.

Five: Schedule your prospecting time. Now that you have your critical and mostly non-negotiable items in your calendar, you need to block out time for *prospecting activities.* We will delve into the details of prospecting in Chapter Eleven, and you will go through some trial and error as you determine how much time you will need to set aside. Just know that you need some dedicated time to dig into your database, follow up with past clients or your sphere of influence, call recently expired listings and properties listed as For Sale by Owner (I suggest you do these daily), and follow up with open house guests.

Six: Deal doctoring. This is the time we spend working *in* our business and not on our business. It should be the area to which you dedicate the smallest amount of time. I am not saying that it isn't critical to your business, but if you develop good systems and work on these items consistently, you should be able to complete the tasks efficiently without letting them become time robbers.

Once you have built your business to a larger scale, these are tasks that should be delegated to an assistant, but in the beginning, you will be taking care of everything yourself. Some agents chose to continue with the administrative activities even after they reach the point where they could hire help. They want to handle their business from "soup to nuts," because that is how they define their services. Again, if it is your decision to do this, that is fine – but that time must be managed, so it doesn't get away from you.

Activities in this category include: Contract negotiation, inspections, photography, answering emails, turning in files to the office, marketing activities, walk throughs, etc.

Seven: Research and appointment prep. Every time you schedule an appointment, you should block out some time *one or two days prior* to that appointment to do research and prepare! Again, this will take less time as you hone your skills and put systems in place, but in the beginning, this can take a significant amount of time – so be sure to allow for it! For sellers, you will need to do a CMA on their home and prepare or customize your listing presentation, and for buyers, you will need to research potential properties and schedule the home tours.

You should find that you have a lot of scheduled activities, but you should also have some free space here and there. When you find a hole in your schedule, this is where you should work on systematizing your business, social media posts and basic organizational activities. This is where you deal with that pile of stuff that is not urgent, but which has been accumulating on your desk or in the back of your mind.

Unscheduled Activities

Here, we deal with the "stuff" that comes at you every day. Things you can't necessarily plan for. The most important and disruptive of these activities is **lead follow up**. When you receive a new lead, it **must** be responded to immediately. Unless you are in an appointment with a client, you should always answer your phone when the caller could be a new lead. The phone call itself shouldn't take more than a few minutes. You find out what the caller is calling about and answer a few basic questions, then schedule an appointment to meet them or to call back later.

I also suggest setting up a *custom auto text* in your phone, so when someone calls, and you can't answer, they receive a text with a message. I suggest something simple that says, "Hi! Sorry I can't talk right now. I will call you right back. In the meantime, you can get information on any of my properties at..." Then, point them to your website.

I want to be clear, I do believe in "The Miracle Morning" concept. I think a good healthy routine in the morning is important to starting your day. I believe that if you take some time for yourself, get your head right and eat a good breakfast, you will be focused and ready for your day.

Not everyone is a morning person, but it is a known fact that our willpower, creativity and energy are stronger in the morning. As the day goes on, we use our willpower, and it depletes. How many times have you put something off until "later," and when "later" comes, you say, "I'll do it in the morning when I'm fresh"? It takes discipline and focus, and you will increase your odds of success by setting the tone in the morning.

I also believe in the "Eat the Frog" concept. This concept suggests that you schedule those things that are the most difficult for you in the morning. Once they are done, you will gain confidence and set the tone for the rest of the day.

I highly recommend *The Miracle Morning: The Not-So-Obvious Secret Guaranteed to Transform Your Life (Before 8 a.m.)*, by Hal Elrod and *Eat That Frog: 21 Great Ways to Stop Procrastinating and Get More Done in Less Time*, by Brian Tracy. In these books, you will learn how a healthy start to your morning can transform your day, and your productivity. Consider: If you were to eat a live frog first thing in the morning, nothing worse can happen to you the rest of the day!

Discipline & Environment

Other important factors in time management are discipline and environment. As I said earlier, for the most part you don't have to answer to anyone other than yourself. In the beginning, you are working on lead generation, and quite often you get no immediate reward. This leads to discouragement, and many people will give up. This discipline is the main reason why 20% of real estate agents are closing 80% of sales.

During times when you become discouraged, you need to look at your vision board or the picture you saved on your phone or computer screen and remember your *Why*. Stay on task and follow your schedule as much as you possibly can.

Your home office is serious business

You need to take a good look at your environment. When I was new to real estate, I set up a home office "space" and sat down at my desk with my coffee in the morning to check emails first thing. That would lead to checking Facebook, and before I knew it, it was 10 a.m., and I hadn't accomplished anything productive! Then I would shower and dress, with intention of looking up those expired listings and knocking on the doors on my way to the office to attend a training being offered at 1 p.m.

But then, I would notice that pile of laundry and the dishes in the sink. I would look for something for breakfast and notice we were low on food, and before I knew it, it was too late to get the office in time to attend that class. I would think, "Oh well, I guess I will hit those expired listings tomorrow. Today, I'll go grocery shopping and get some laundry done." The next day I would actually get *angry* when I saw that expired listing re-listed with a competitor! How dare they not wait for me!

As much as possible, put yourself in an environment without distractions. When you can, go to the office first thing in the morning. If you don't have office space outside of home, then try to make yourself a defined office with a door. If that isn't possible, then you must create your atmosphere mentally. Your work hours are work hours and no household chores can be done during that time.

Minimizing Distractions

You need to minimize distractions. When you are completing a defined task, let's say, you're preparing for a listing appointment that you have in a few days, what are the things that might pull you away from that task? Is it a co-worker wanting to chat, your kids, a phone call or an important email? There are things that you can do to prevent these disruptions.

Set expectations so you can focus

Set *expectations* with the people around you so they know that when you are sitting at your desk working on something, you are not to be disturbed. When you take a break and are up from your desk, that is when it's time to chat. Even more important is setting those expectations with the people at home. Tell them, "Work time is *work time*, and unless someone is dead or bleeding, please wait until I am done to ask me that question."

When I was managing a busy real estate office, I put a sign on my door that said, "I am working on something time sensitive and cannot be disturbed. Please send me a text if you need to see me, and I will reach out as soon as I am done." This was the 21st century method of "taking a number," so people didn't feel like they needed to hang around outside my door when I was on the phone.

Set limits on technology

Distractions don't always come from people anymore, do they? You also need to turn off the notifications that are constantly coming at you throughout the day. I figured out several years ago that I rarely need my phone to make any noise at all. I look at my phone often enough that if I received a phone call, email or text, I will know about it soon enough and be able to respond.

If I am free to receive a call, then I turn my phone on and the only things on my phone that make sound are calls and texts. There is no audible notification for emails or private messages. This helps me take control and manage when to respond to these disruptions. When you hear that constant bing ... it causes anxiety and makes you rush through your tasks so you can address the noise that is happening around you.

Turn off the noise and focus on the work at hand.

> *Activity* is not *productivity*.
> Busy-ness rarely takes care of business.

Deliberate Scheduling Reflects Your Success

The fact that your time is flexible is one of things that probably attracted you to real estate. And it can be very beneficial, as long as you take control of your schedule instead of letting your schedule control you. Your activity should be deliberate! Be sure to schedule some down time for yourself so that you can maintain a work/life balance.

How much you work directly impacts your bottom line, so the amount of discipline you apply should be directly related to your goals. If you only want to sell 10 homes a year, then you won't have to apply as much discipline as if you want to sell 50 homes a year. It's all up to you and completely within your control.

Every Day Action Item:

Every night before you go to bed, check your schedule for tomorrow. Be sure you have a plan and that your activities are deliberate. Write out your to-do list and lock in the commitment to stick to it.

EVERY DAY AGENT

Chapter Seven: Contact Management – Keep Friends Close & Everyone Else Closer

Get Organized (I'm going to help.)

The first thing to consider is your contact management program or CRM (Contact Relationship Manager). There are tons of different programs out there, and it is possible that your brokerage provides one for you. The important thing is to find one that will work for you and **use it**.

I started in real estate before the existence of all the fancy automated programs. Don't get me wrong – we did have computers and an MLS system – but business systems have come a long way, and the proper use of them can be very beneficial. When I started, my contacts were in about five different places. I had people in MLS on drip campaigns, I had lists of people who came in to open houses, I had people in my Gmail contacts, and the company I worked for had a lead capture program that funneled prospects into my CRM when they inquired about a particular property. I always felt a little fragmented when it came to managing this part of my business, so when I started using an all-in-one CRM program, it was a game changer!

Do you have any idea how many people you have saved in your phone contacts? How about your email contact list? Take a look – the number might surprise you! I have 907 contacts in my cell phone. When I first looked at that number, I was shocked. That contact list is GOLD, and I have not been taking proper advantage of it.

> **Did you know:** *About 65% of your business will come from people you know?*

The trick to making it work is to put everyone into one system that helps manage your interactions with them.

We call the people you know your Sphere of Influence (SOI) or Center of Influence. It is very disappointing when you find out that a friend, neighbor or relative just put their home on the market or purchased a home without calling you – and it happens. All. The. Time!!

The average person knows about **seven** real estate agents. So, it's up to you to be sure you are top of mind to as many people as possible.

Choosing A Great CRM

Your CRM should be the catch-all place to enter and manage everyone. When you hold an open house, enter the people you met that day. If you go to a party and meet three new people, enter them in your CRM. Your holiday card list? Yup – them, too. Everyone you know, everyone you meet and everyone you've ever done business with, goes in the CRM.

When selecting a CRM, consider these key functions.

- Your online lead generation should funnel directly to your CRM. So, for example, when a consumer is looking at homes online and finds your web\site, they should be prompted to sign in. This should then immediately alert you that you have a new lead and put that lead directly into your CRM.

- Your CRM should have an automatic campaign function which allows you to "set it and forget it" – to an extent.

- You should be able to easily manage your contacts from anywhere. It should be web-based and have mobile functionality – so you can call people at the push of a button and update activity easily from anywhere.

- You should be able to easily import and export contacts in and out of your CRM. When you are in the initial set-up process, you can take all your phone contacts, email contacts, MLS contacts etc., and import them into your system. If you ever change CRM programs, or change brokerages where the CRM belongs to them, you want to be able to easily export your contacts out of the program.

Using your CRM daily is vital to its effectiveness. Remember that prospecting time that you scheduled into your calendar in the Chapter Six section, "How to build your calendar"? Having a good CRM will make that time productive and deliberate. You should be able to login and immediately have a list of people to call. It might be past clients whom you check-in with from time to time (and ask for referrals!) or follow-up calls from an open house. Whatever it is, you won't be in a position where you sit and think, "Who should I call today? Where am I going to get business?"

Systematize your database, and your database will work for you!

Every Day Action Item:

Challenge yourself to add five (5) new contacts to your CRM every day. Once you add them, put them on an action plan with either a reminder for your next contact or a property drip campaign.

EVERY DAY AGENT

Chapter Eight: Market Knowledge – Be A Local Resource

Part of your scheduled activity must include advancing your local market knowledge. When you are new, one of the most useful things you can do with your time includes looking at homes on the market. Participate in broker tours, if you have them in your area, or pair up with an agent in the office and preview homes when it is practical to do so. You want to avoid making appointments to see occupied homes, because that can be an inconvenience to the occupant. But you can identify the vacant homes on the market and tour these homes to your heart's content.

Clearly, you can't begin to see every home that is on the market. That would be impractical. But making it a point to see as many as you can does have a few key benefits.

Benefits of Market Research

First, it helps you "talk the talk." Let's say you are holding an open house in a particular neighborhood on Sunday. The week before, you should plan to see every home in that area that is currently on the market. That way, when people come into your open house, you can talk about the other homes available in the area with confidence, because you have seen them first-hand. Looking them up online is one thing – actually having been in them gives you much more credibility to talk about them.

Second, you benefit from the sheer practice of looking at homes. When you finally get that first buyer in your car, you don't want it to be the first time you have navigated through the process of showing a home. Trust me, there are complications that will arise during this process that you can't begin to prepare for – but you can get good at troubleshooting by gaining some experience.

Ask anyone who has been in the real estate business for a while about their "horror stories" from showing property. You will hear everything from finding people asleep in their beds to aggressive dogs, to doors that won't open or close... or lock...or unlock ... I think you get the picture.

After almost two decades in the business, there is pretty much no door that I can't figure out how to open or close – it's a practiced art! The last thing you want to do is look like an idiot, because you can't figure out how to unlock the sliding glass door that leads to the lanai. A little practice and experience go a long way to help you look like a pro.

Use the MLS

When it comes to market knowledge, one of the best tools you can use is the MLS. I suggest you set up an auto email within your chosen market area. You should be alerted immediately to all activity in that area. New listings, pending, sold, cancelled or expired – any status changes in your market area should be sent to you. It may seem overwhelming, but you will find that a quick glance at that activity when it pops up will sink in more than you think.

For Example:
I have an auto search set up for the neighborhood where I live. Whenever there is activity, I receive an email with a link to that property in MLS. I click on the link and scan the details. Then, when I am out for a walk, and I run into a neighbor (who, of course knows that I am a real estate agent), I can say "Hey, did you see that house down the street went under con tract? You know, the big one on the lake? It was on the market only 15 days, and it looks like it is supposed to close next week. I'll keep you posted and let you know what it sold for!" Knowing the details of this activity helps establish you as an expert, and it also brings up other talking points.

Let's say someone responds, "Wow! Only 15 days on the market? Things are really selling fast!" Then, you can jump in and assess their interest level with a response like, "You know, there are **no** other homes on the lake on the market right now. Have you thought of selling? Looks like it would be a good time! I'm happy to come over and give you a current price analysis – no obligation."

New construction neighborhoods

If you have new construction neighborhoods in your area, this can be a gold mine for your business plan! I suggest touring each of these communities and getting on their mailing list. If you have a large number of new home communities, like I do in my area, you can schedule one or two new communities per week. Take your time, get to know the inventory – home sizes, price range, community amenities, and other details.

Get to know the sales team! When you get to know the sales team, there are a couple of immediate benefits.

First, new construction sales teams are more willing to work with you when you have a buyer. Each builder has their own guidelines when it comes to paying your commission. Most of them have something that says if you don't accompany the buyer and introduce them to the community on their first visit, then they don't have to pay your commission. Of course, you want to accompany them whenever possible, but if they are out driving around on their own and stumble into a new model home community, you want to have an arrangement in place, so you don't lose the commission.

Establish a relationship with the sales team, so they know you are working as a business partner who brings buyers to their neighborhood. Then, they may be more open to a quick phone call introduction or even open to having a buyer show up and present your business card to indicate your relationship with them.

Second, new home communities are often negotiating with buyers who need to sell their current homes in order to buy a home in the new neighborhood. If you are the sales team's go-to business partner, they might refer clients to you to list their homes. Especially if you can assure the sales team that you will do a great job and sell the house fast, so they can move forward with the new home purchase! It's a win-win relationship!

Introducing buyers to new home communities can be some of the easiest money you'll ever make! Get to know these opportunities and be ready to help your clients navigate through the complicated process, and it will be money in the bank!

Every Day Action Item:

Set up an auto search for one neighborhood in your market area. Make an appointment to see all the active houses in that area (if possible) and visit at least one new construction neighborhood each week (if applicable).

EVERY DAY AGENT

Chapter Nine: Contract Knowledge – Proceed with Caution

The funny thing about getting a real estate license – and I've heard this over and over again – is that after all the hours of school and two grueling exams, you really have no idea how to sell real estate! You would have expected, at the very least, for the class to cover the state contract, right? *Wrong.*

You might be an expert in calculating prorations, and you may know how many square feet are in an acre, but you may never have laid eyes on a state real estate contract. Depending on personality, some people get really caught up on this, and some just jump in and wing it.

I caution you against doing either.

My message to you when it comes to the contract:

While you *do* need to know what you are asking clients to obligate themselves to, you don't need to know it "word for word" in the beginning. I have had agents take so much time in the beginning trying to understand every word of our 13-page contract that it paralyzes them, and they never even get to the point of needing to use it.

Contract Classes

Your brokerage, local association and often local real estate attorneys are all places you can look for contract classes. When you first get licensed and join a brokerage, get your hands on a copy of the contract and listing agreement. Read through these agreements with the eyes of a buyer or seller. Think about what you would want to know if you were the one signing it and *highlight the things you don't understand.* Then, attend a few classes, making sure those questions get answered.

In all my years as a real estate agent, and even now as a broker, I will tell you that there are still occasions where I have to reference a particular clause in our contract in order to apply the language to a particular situation and decide what it means to the parties involved. There are situations that aren't common everyday occurrences, and there is no shame in asking your broker how to handle them.

Story from an Every Day Agent: *"Well, it's on fire."*

My very first weekend as a managing broker, my contract knowledge was tested. It was Saturday morning, and I received a call from one of my agents. She said, "Remember that listing I just put under contract yesterday? Well, it's currently on fire!" She was literally standing in front of the house watching them put out the fire. My brain quickly went to work with the details. There are two clauses in our contract that deal with this situation, but I couldn't recall every detail. I told her I'd call her back.

I pulled up the contract on my computer. I read the two clauses that address this particular situation to understand the obligations and options of each party, then took it from there. In the end, the buyer *did* complete the purchase of the house, about eight months later. It turns out, the fire was set by the disgruntled tenant, who was not happy about having to move. The seller's homeowner's insurance covered the cost of the repairs, and once the repairs were done and the home was put back to its original condition, the transaction came to a successful close.

You will have situations come up in this business that you don't know how to handle. You will either need to have a broker that you can go to for help, or perhaps a real estate attorney if you work independently. The state association might also have a hotline you can call for answers to specific questions about the contract.

Please don't wing it when it comes to your contract knowledge – the stakes are way too high for you and your clients. But at the same time, don't let your lack of experience stop you from moving forward. The only way you are going to learn is by *doing*, so get out there and do it, with guidance and supervision, and your knowledge will grow with each transaction.

Every Day Action Item:

Pick a partner (co-worker, spouse etc.) and pretend they have identified a home they would like to buy. Write up the offer with them, as you would with a buyer client. Then, practice presenting that offer to your partner, who pretends to be the buyer. Do this with the listing agreement, and role play with someone as if they were the seller. Change up the scenarios to utilize different addenda. For example, try adding special circumstances, like a "home to sell contingency" or "the house is in an age-restricted community."

EVERY DAY AGENT

EVERY DAY AGENT

Chapter Ten: Process Management – Get Your Ducks in a Row

Whether you are with an established real estate office, or with an independent brokerage, you will need to have some basic systems and programs in place in order to navigate through your day-to-day business. We already discussed the CRM, which will be your most important tool – but you will also need to have an e-signature program, file management, marketing programs and the like. These are going to differ greatly given your particular situation, but here are some things you need to think about, so you are most prepared when things start to get busy!

In my introduction to this book, I recalled the panic that set in the moment my first buyer told me they were ready to make an offer! No matter how much you have studied the contract, you are going to feel lost when it's time to write that offer, unless you are prepared. In my many years of selling and managing, there were things that came up on a regular basis that I thought should be systematized, but no one had seemed to take the time to do it.

For example, when asked to write that offer, if I had a document prepared that outlined all the details needed to make that offer, I wouldn't have felt that fear. In fact, I would have appeared to be experienced, professional and prepared.

Below I will outline the key things you must have in place in order to provide a professional experience for your client and keep your sanity at the same time.

Every Day Agent Resource: Buyer Interview Sheet

Ideally, you should work with your broker or an experienced agent on this – but if that is not available to you, then you will have to go it alone. Take your state real estate contract and go line by line, page by page. Every time there is something that needs to be filled in, create an interview question for that item. Continue until you have outlined all the information needed to make an offer. This information will vary by state, but generally, you will need to know:

✓ The full legal names of all the parties and how they want to take title to the property.
✓ Current contact information including email addresses if using an e-sig nature program.

- ✓ The property address and legal description.
- ✓ Will they be paying cash or financing? (You may need pre-approval or proof of funds).
- ✓ If financing, what type of financing and what are the terms? (For ex: Down payment, interest rate, etc.).
- ✓ Offer amount.
- ✓ Escrow amount.
- ✓ Closing date.
- ✓ Time needed for inspections or other due diligence.
- ✓ Repair limits.
- ✓ Items included in the purchase.
- ✓ Items excluded from the purchase.
- ✓ Will either party be providing a home warranty?

Plus, any additional terms that might be relevant in your particular area.

When your client is ready to make an offer, you pull this document up on your computer or phone or whip a printed copy out of your briefcase – whatever the case may be – and go through the terms line by line. Then you can prepare the offer in private and either meet up with them later or send it to them for review and e-signature.

Every Day Agent Resources: Accepted Offer/Key Dates Emails to Clients & Other Agents

Want to guarantee a smooth transaction and be someone who everyone wants to work with, while also offering **great** service to your client? Implement this simple step in every transaction.

Email to other agents

Once you have an accepted and ratified contract, send an email to the other agent. It doesn't matter which side of the transaction you are on, chances are, the other agent isn't going to do it. The email should include the key dates and any other action items that are expected from any of the parties. Put it all in writing up front and the chance of something getting missed or miscommunicated is significantly decreased. My email would look something like this:

Hi Agent,

Thank you for working with me on getting this contract together. I look forward to working with you. I have attached the signed contract package and have noted all the key dates and obligations below. Please reply to this with your agreement to these dates and terms.

Agreement Item	Date (example)
The contract effective date is:	*02-19-2019*
Escrow deposit is due to be deposited with XYZ Title Company by:	*02-22-2019*
Buyer to complete loan application by:	*02-25-2019*
The seller selected XYZ Title for the closing, please provide them with a copy of the contract.	
Buyer inspection is scheduled for 10 a.m.	*02-22-2019*
Please confirm with seller.	
Buyer will have loan approval by:	*03-21-2019*
Closing date is scheduled for:	*03-28-2019*
Seller to provide a home warranty per contract.	

Thank you again for your assistance, I look forward to a successful closing.

Sincerely,
Great Agent

This email could also include items such as the buyer providing their application to a homeowner or condo association, a home-to-sell contingency, seller concessions or any other terms that require timely action or response.

Making this a regular practice will make a huge difference in the flow of your business. When it comes to complicated real estate transactions, communication is key. You need to be sure you keep track of the action items required on your end. The best way to ensure that everything gets done when it's supposed to is by creating a contract-to-closing checklist and plugging all the key dates into some sort of reminder system.

Email to clients

A similar email can be sent to your client, outlining the key dates and action items that pertain to their obligations in the contract. It would look something like this:

> *Hello Client,*
>
> *Congratulations on the (purchase or sale) of your home! I have attached a fully executed copy of the purchase agreement. I will keep in touch with you every step of the way, but I wanted to outline the key dates, so you plan accordingly...*

Then outline for them the key dates and obligations that apply to them, including escrow deposit, loan application, arranging for inspections, etc.

Every Day Agent Resource: Contract-to-Closing Checklist

Similar to the buyer interview, create a timeline and checklist to keep track of each step between contract and closing. This checklist is much more involved than the Interview Sheet or Key Dates email, as it will cover all your required action item steps from contract to closing.

When working with a buyer, the most important thing to remember about the contract-to-closing process is protecting your client's escrow deposit. You need to keep track of each contract milestone and make sure they are addressing each item within the timeframe set forth in the contract.

Some of the items covered include:

- ✓ Your brokerage's required paperwork and turning in the file to the office.
- ✓ Confirming the escrow deposit has been made.
- ✓ If applicable, confirming the buyer has initiated their loan application.
- ✓ Arranging and attending inspections and negotiating repair items within appropriate time frame.
- ✓ Ordering home warranty.
- ✓ Sending an executed contract to the closing company and/or lender.
- ✓ Arranging for pre-closing walk through.
- ✓ Reviewing all closing documents and turning final paperwork into the office.

✓ Sending information to your client about the closing process – including what to bring to closing, expectations on the day of closing, transfer of utilities, and other details.

You will need a separate checklist for when you are working with a seller than when you are working with a buyer, as the obligations are different. Also, things can often change during the process, so be sure to keep those lines of communication open.

For example, a price adjustment may be made after inspections or appraisal. That addendum needs to be signed by all parties and provided to the closing agent and the lender. Sometimes there is a change in the closing date, which can cause a domino effect that changes several steps in the process.

Every Day Agent Resource: New Listing Checklist

Similar to the Contract-to-Closing Checklist, you will want to create a checklist to cover all the steps involved when you take a new listing. In addition to the necessary paperwork, you will need to look after many moving parts, and it's best to have a process to follow, so nothing gets missed.

Some items on this checklist include:

✓ Seller disclosures completed and signed.
✓ Home preparation items.
✓ Schedule photography.
✓ Installation of signage.
✓ Obtain a key and arrange access to property (usually with a lock box). Discuss showing instructions, including any alarm codes or gate codes.
✓ Measure rooms.
✓ Enter into MLS system.
✓ Marketing – create property flyer, post in social media, create ads, property web exposure, etc.
✓ Arrange the Open House and/or broker tour.

Again, I recommend sending an initial email to the seller(s), outlining what they need to do, confirming how showings will be handled and what to expect moving forward. Find out their preferred method of communication and determine the main point of contact. Arrange for regularly scheduled communication – weekly at minimum, but more often if needed.

File Management

Much of this topic depends greatly on your individual situation. Your brokerage will most likely have a very defined process for turning in files, and your system will be determined by those requirements. As a new agent, it is critical that you follow the process in place and get your paperwork turned into the office as soon as possible. With most brokerages, the documents will be reviewed by a staff member or manager/broker, and any missing items will be identified. This process is in place to protect you and the client, and it is a step that should not be overlooked or delayed.

It is also critical that you organize documents in a way that you can easily access them, from anywhere. In our business, it is often likely that someone will call you in desperate need of a document while you are away from the office. If you have a file management system that allows you to access your files from your phone, you would be able to get that document where it needs to be with ease. There are apps that fulfill this purpose as well as web-based programs – either of these will work in this situation.

Tips to get & stay organized

If you don't have a program that keeps your files for you, here is a suggestion:

Make a folder on your desktop called "Real Estate". Inside this folder, make two subfolders, one titled Buyers and one titled Sellers. Each time you have a transaction (for me, this meant a signed/ratified contract or listing agreement), create a folder with the property address as the name of the file. The reason I did not use the client's name is because I would often have multiple transactions with one client, or you could have two clients with the same last name at the same time. Save all files pertaining to this transaction inside that folder for ease of access.

There are many applications out there to allow access to these files from a web browser or cloud storage, such as iCloud, Google Docs, Dropbox, Box, SugarSync or Sharepoint.

A similar system should be put in place for emails pertaining to a particular transaction. You can do this in a few ways. Your email program should allow you to create folders, in which case you could follow the same format above within your email program and save emails into the appropriate folder as you get them. Or, you can save emails as PDFs and put them into the transaction folder that you created.

These electronic files should be backed up and kept for seven (7) years in case you need to access them.

Pro Tip:

> At tax time, send an electronic copy of the closing statement to each of your clients who closed transactions in the last year. Drop a quick note saying you were just thinking of them, and you thought they might need this document for their taxes. Then, ask them for referrals! Include something like:
>
> "It was such a pleasure working with you, and I'd love to be able to offer your friends and family the same great service. Of the people you know, who do you think is most likely to have a real estate need coming up?"

Every Day Agent Resource & Action Item: Upgrade your checklists

Create your own documents based on your contract and business specifics.
For templates of the following documents that you can use, visit the resource section at EverydayREAgent.com:

- ✓ *Buyer Offer Interview Form*
- ✓ *Key Dates Email*
- ✓ *Contract-to-Closing Checklist*
- ✓ *Seller Checklist*

Now that you are feeling knowledgeable and organized, it's time to get into the "meat and potatoes" of *growing* your business. I know: "prospecting" can be a word that instills fear in your heart and brings up all kinds of anxiety. But I promised I would give you reality and help you focus on five income-generating activities, right? So, let's get into it!

EVERY DAY AGENT

PART THREE – THE MEAT AND POTATOES

If you are not familiar with the concept of "spinning plates," it is a metaphor for balancing many activities at once. In real estate, the amount of potential revenue-generating activities out there can be very overwhelming. I found that narrowing it down to a manageable and effective list of activities has a two-tiered effect.

First, it allows you to focus and takes the fear out of the whole process. When you think of "prospecting," what is the first thing that comes to mind? Cold calling, knocking on doors and memorizing scripts. If these things are outside of your comfort zone – like they are for most people – chances are, you will find excuses not to do them.

Second, it allows you to hone your skills and excel at these select activities, which makes them more effective.

Earlier, I told you that I would show you how to focus on just five activities that will build your real estate business. I used this strategy myself with great success, and I have coached many agents over the years who have built their businesses on this foundation as well.

I can't tell you how many times I have seen a frustrated, distraught agent in my office, telling me they don't know what else they can be doing! The scene plays out the same almost every time. I look across the desk and say, "I am going to give you a list of five activities. You can do five things, right? If you do these five things consistently, your business will grow. Do you want to know what they are?"

They stare at me and nod with anticipation. Then I say, "You'll want to write this down".

Chapter Eleven – Open Houses & Floor Time

Open Houses: More Than A Plate of Cookies

One of the best things you can do when starting out is host open houses, as long as you do them right. I can't tell you how many times I have gone into an "Open House," being held by an agent, only to find them sitting in a corner, reading a book. They glance up and say, "Hello. Feel free to have a look around, and let me know if you have any questions," and proceed to read their book or look at their phone.

Not every experience is like this, but there are more than you would think. I have also had the experience of asking a question, only to find out they are not prepared with the answer. You don't have to know everything about the house or the neighborhood, but you should know the basics and have access to additional information.

In this chapter, I am going to dispel some well-known myths and show you how to conduct an Open House that gets maximum results.

Myth #1 – You can't do an open house if you don't have any listings

You don't need your own listings, as long as you are with a company or office that has listings. If you are on your own, then that is a different story. But, as long as you are in a thriving, productive office, there will be opportunities.

Many new agents ask if I can send out an email to all the agents to announce that they are available to hold open houses. I advise them to approach it differently. I tell them to go into MLS and search for the office's active listings. Then, they can filter by neighborhood and price point.

As an agent, you should *choose* the Open Houses you hold. If given a choice, other agents are going to give you their less-desirable scenarios. You want to select a house that is in an area where you want to work, and one that is easily accessible to the public. Homes that take 15 turns off the main road, or those in gated communities, will receive far less traffic than homes close to the main road.

Try to select the homes that will have the most impact on your business, then reach out to the listing agent and offer to do an open house for them.

It's important that you have some experience behind you and that you can reassure the listing agent that you will do a great job. (More on this later!)

Myth #2 – Potential buyers who come in the door are already working with an agent.

When I start hearing this type of general negativity, it makes me crazy! If this is your mindset, then you are going to need a serious attitude adjustment in order to be successful in this business. Every open house is an opportunity, and I am going to show you how to optimize your results. Not every open house will deliver ready, willing, and able prospects to your door, but real estate is a numbers game. The more open houses you do, the better your odds.

Myth #3 – Buyers don't want to give out their contact information.

Again, so much negativity! People may be hesitant to give up their contact information, but with a few clever strategies, you increase your odds significantly. First, they have to *like* and *trust* you, and second, they have to get something in return. Everyone, and I mean *everyone*, when talking to a salesperson is thinking in the back of their head, "What's in it for me?" Sometimes, this is referred to as the "WIIFM factor" for a buyer.

Now that we have set these negative thoughts aside, let's talk about how to get the most out of your open houses.

Of course, when you begin to have your own listings, you will have plenty of opportunities for open houses. Try to schedule them a few weeks in advance, if you can. If you schedule your Open House a few weeks out, it gives you optimum time to leverage the event and get the word out. I know this isn't possible in all markets, as some homes won't stay on the market that long. You *must* hit those during their first week on the market!

Advertising for an Open House

If you work for a brokerage that does **newspaper advertising** (believe it or not, some still do, and it can be very effective!), then be sure your open house is scheduled to be in the paper that weekend.

Schedule the open house **in the MLS** as well. In most cases, open house information will syndicate out to other real estate websites that highlight open houses, such as realtor.com and Zillow.

Create an ad for your **social media**, then run it as much as you can leading up to the event. The ad should be simple and eye catching. When someone clicks on it, the link should lead them to the home's information on your website. I have seen agents grab the Zillow URL from the listing and put that link on their Facebook ad. The problem with doing this is that *Zillow captures the lead and sells it back to you!*

If **your website** has an IDX feed from your MLS, search your own website for any property that you currently have listed. Copy the URL from your own website to use for your Facebook or other social media ads. Don't forget about LinkedIn, Instagram and Twitter. Get the word out in every way available.

If **NextDoor** is in your area, it is another great place to advertise open houses. There are sections of NextDoor where you can advertise appropriately, but don't do it on the general discussion site. Be sure to follow all social media sites' advertising guidelines.

A word about forums and online neighborhood groups

A lot of agents ask if I think they should join an online neighborhood group (such as NextDoor or other similar platforms) in order to promote themselves and their listings. I think that in many forums, people don't want the neighborhood real estate agent constantly trying to sell their services. What I suggest is to join as their neighbor and be helpful in very specific and appropriate ways.

Be the person who always has the answer others are looking for. When someone asks, "Does anyone know what is going up on the corner of Elm and Main Street?" you should be the one to answer with the information. You don't need a sales pitch, just be helpful. They will remember you when they do have a real estate need.

Sign every post with your name and brokerage, so everyone knows where to find you. Remind them – right next to your name – that you are, indeed, a real estate professional.

Word of Mouth Marketing: Knock or Call Around the Listing

Disclaimer on this strategy: You should only do this if:
    1) it is your listing, *or*
    2) you have the permission of the listing agent to do it.

The last thing you want to do is run over the agent who you are holding the open house for. If you do, you will never get the opportunity again, I guarantee it. However, if it is your listing or you have their blessing, then you should always take advantage of the opportunity to meet some neighbors.

Call or knock on their door with a purpose. You will want to have done some research and have general information about market activity in their specific neighborhood. Simply say that you are holding an Open House, give them the address and a date and time that is reserved *exclusively for the neighbors*. Ask if they know anyone looking to move to the neighborhood and show them your market report. **Don't give it to them, only show it to them.**

Your market report should be a professional, visually pleasing, easy-to-read, one or two-page document that shows recent activity. Check with your brokerage or your MLS to see if they have a program for this. It should be something that any homeowner would *want* to have. Once they have looked at it, offer to email one to them every month – no obligation and no spam! You will just send the report once a month. Tell them you look forward to seeing them at the Open House, remind them of the address, date and time, then leave.

If no one is home when you knock, have a door hanger with an invitation to the Open House and a sample of your market report, including a call to action. A good closing line is something like, "To receive this report once every month (no obligations and no spam!), send me an email at: ..." Then, include your email address.

Remember, if you want to *get* something (in this case, their email address), you have to *give* something of value.

-

Signage Makes (or Breaks) Your Open House Traffic

Many agents put signs out the day before the Open House. Depending on local custom and area regulations, I don't think this is a bad idea. The most important thing is that you don't skimp on this step. Don't be a lazy realtor. Get out there in advance of the event and put out as many signs as you can. Put them on the main intersections leading to the neighborhood, then lead drivers to the house from all directions.

One of my biggest pet peeves is when I see Open House signs at a busy intersection, and the words are so small you can't read anything! Often, you can't tell which direction to go to get to the Open House from where the sign is. If you are going to the trouble of buying signs and putting them out, you might as well make them work for you.

Every time someone sees your name, it is another drop in the bucket of personal promotion. You want people to see your name everywhere, to see that you do a lot of business in a particular area, right? Open House signs are an inexpensive, effective way to accomplish this – so don't skimp. Have professional signs made and make them a substantial size. Not obnoxious, but big enough that they can be easily read by someone sitting in a car.

A good Open House sign says, "Open House," then has your name and brokerage, with an arrow. Check with your broker for any regulations or identity standards that may be required by your particular brokerage, and always follow state law when it comes to real estate signage.

If you put out signs in advance of the event, it is critical that you put the day and time on the sign. This can be done using a rider, rather than having that information on the main sign panel. Also, I know it is tempting to put your phone number on the sign, but I don't think it's necessary. The purpose of the sign is to lead them to your Open House. The only reason for a phone number on the sign is if there is a chance that they might not find the house and need to call for directions. If you do a good job with directional arrows, this won't be a problem.

The main things to keep in mind are that everything on your sign should be clear and visible from a distance, and that the signs should lead the consumer to the Open House. Everything else is just a waste of space.

Open House Preparation is "Key": Prepare to Have a Successful Day

When you identify a house that you are going to hold open, you *must* do some research in preparation for the event. If it's your listing, then you should already know the most essential information, such as community fees, amenities and taxes, as well as the features of the home itself.

If it is not your listing, then these are things you should get to know.

Know the neighborhood

I also recommend that you do a quick search of recent activity in the neighborhood. Go preview any homes that are currently on the market. This way, if you engage in conversation with someone at the Open House and there is a particular feature they are looking for in a home, you can offer your personal insight.

For example, maybe they say they are looking for a spacious office – it's one of their "hot buttons." Luckily, you visited a house down the street that has a nice-sized office. You can tell them about that house and ask them if you can schedule a showing for them.

If you hadn't physically previewed that home, you might not have known that key information. Be in the know, and you will gain rapport with your visitors.

"Should I serve refreshments?"

Whether or not you serve refreshments at your Open Houses is completely up to you. I was always an "outside the box" thinker when it came to that kind of thing. I've always liked to do things that stood out, rather than just a boring plate of cookies and bottled water.

One time, when it was really cold outside, I served hot chocolate with marshmallows. This won't necessarily bring more people in, because they won't know about it until they get there, but it will be memorable. It also might cause guests to stick around a little longer.

Along the same lines, there was one day that it was extremely hot outside, so I had ice cream sandwiches in the freezer. Something easy that guests could hold in their hand, and who doesn't like a cool, refreshing ice cream sandwich?

It doesn't have to be fancy, but you can do something thoughtful that sets you apart. Another tactic I have used is providing a grab-and-go bag of snacks. Most people touring Open Houses are driving around looking at houses for hours, which can turn into a long day with little time or opportunity for breaks. Pack a brown bag with a small bottle of water, some chips, crackers or granola bar, an apple and a piece of candy. Of course, you will want to include some branding on and in the bag. Then, it's something they take with them and appreciate all day!

Every Day Agent Resource: Open House Toolbox

Now, let's talk about your Open House toolbox. What should you have with you when you conduct an Open House? When I was selling, I had my realtor tool kit in the trunk of my car at all times. This contained:

✓ window cleaner	✓ plates	✓ small broom	✓ paperclips
✓ paper towels	✓ cups	✓ scissors	✓ business cards
✓ trash bags	✓ napkins	✓ zip ties	✓ hand sanitizer
✓ cutlery	✓ pens		

This is more than an Open House tool kit; it is your real estate tool kit! You should have these items at hand all the time.

Pro Tip:

Whenever you prepare to show a house, whether it's an Open House, broker open, or just a showing, you should always arrive first and do a walk through. Flush toilets, wipe down sinks or counter tops, freshen up the entrance with a quick sweep, remove dead bugs (sorry, but it's part of the job!), and turn on the lights.

Bring minimal marketing materials

Those are the tools you should have at hand, but what about handouts, market information, brochures, and the like? This is where my opinion might be a little unconventional, so stay with me and follow my logic.

The two points of the Open House are to create relationships with people who are looking to buy a house, *and* to impress neighbors who are thinking about selling. My strategy was to do everything in my power to get the contact information of everyone who came in the door. This can be very difficult.

You have about 30 seconds to make a good impression, so how are you going to stand out? I will say that you aren't going to win everyone over. There are millions of people out there and millions of personalities. Some people just don't mesh. Often, when people go to open houses, they are shopping for a real estate agent. They may or may not know it, but they are. Either they need help and haven't met an agent they want to work with yet, or they think they don't need help and are trying to do it on their own. In either case, it's your job to show them that you will bring value to them. Show them that they need to work with you.

So, my strategy is to provide *as little written information about the property as possible*. **What?** No long-winded property feature sheets or expensive color brochures?

No and no.

At least, not anything that they can take with them without talking to you first. Some people will do anything to avoid talking to you. It's not personal, but no one likes a salesperson. And, they do not want you to have their phone number or email. So, if there is a brochure or property flyer on the counter, they will grab one and run out the door, avoiding any conversation or exchange of information.

Have a winning house information book

Have a professional-looking book, something well put together and bound, for them to look at while touring the property. It should include all information about the house, community and a little about you. (More on what this book should contain later.) Then, have a few take-away marketing pieces tucked in your briefcase, but not out where anyone can just grab one.

Display top selling points & house information

Make some very professional signs to display around the house, describing its key features. These can be set on tables or displayed on a wall near a doorway. You must be sure never to damage a wall, and there are Lucite displays with backing that adheres securely and removes completely without damage. Always have the seller's permission before adhering anything to the wall. Put some personality into the wording on the signs. Make them colorful. Be sure they are in plain sight, easy to read, and provide helpful information. At least a few of them should have a call to action, such as, "Ask me about the insulation upgrade in the attic."

There also should be signs directing guests how to get more information about this or *any house on the market*. Here is where a little technology comes in to play. There are a few ways you can accomplish this, and how you do it is up to you, your level of technical ability, and what is available to you through your brokerage.

There's an app for that – use it!

Most large brokerages have a dedicated property search app, which would be perfect in this situation. The one that I had available to me only required that a consumer text my name to a short code, and they received a link. Then, they could save that link on their phone, and anytime they wanted information about any property, they could open the app and search by location, address or an MLS number.

The beauty of it for me is that as soon as they texted my name to the short code, I captured their cell phone number. In addition, the app allows me to see the properties they look at. So, with this magic app in my arsenal, I made a flyer that told Open House visitors they could receive information about any home on the market, then provided my name and short code they should send a text to.

Never underestimate the value of free QR codes

If you don't have a property search app available to you, you could direct people to your website, but this isn't quite as effective. If you have the ability to use a QR Code, which is an encoded image that they can scan with their phone, use a QR Code to direct them to your website. This greatly increases the effectiveness. People are more likely to take out their phone and send a text to get information, or snap a picture of a QR code, than they are to type in a web URL.

And, even if they do type in the web URL, they may not ever register on your website. You won't even capture them as a lead! Instead, make it quick and easy to for them to get the information they are looking for and for you to capture their contact information at the same time.

Collecting visitor information – the old-fashioned ask

If you don't have these capabilities, or you're not comfortable with this strategy, then my final suggestion is to ask them for their contact information directly when they ask you for property information. Immediately after the Open House, email them a full brochure of the property.

I simply used to tell people that I am saving trees by not having a ton of wasted printed materials. Also, always assure them that you will not sell their email or spam them. Simply send them what they have asked for.

Handling Traffic Flow and Creating Meaningful Relationships

Probably the most challenging part of holding an Open House is getting people to talk to you. As I said before, they are going to avoid talking to you as much as possible, and you are going to have to push yourself outside your comfort zone.

Strategies for handling Open House traffic flow

Keep in mind that, sometimes, you will have tons of people walking through at once (as a result of all the great advertising and promotion you did!), and sometimes, you will have only one or two groups the whole day.

Position yourself where people will see you when they walk in the door. Say, "Hello and welcome!" Some will come to where you are, in which case, you can tell them, "Feel free to look around. Come back and see me before you leave." Maybe let them know you have refreshments.

While they tour the house, listen in on their conversation. If they are alone, you can note which areas they linger in.

Look for anything on them that might be a conversation starter – a sports cap, brand logo on their T-shirt, etc. As they finish up their tour, position yourself between them and the exit, and ask if they have any questions.

Then, you should ask them some questions. You are trying to uncover their particular situation and what needs you can offer solutions for. Avoid going into a sales pitch or telling them you can help them find a house if this one didn't work for them.

Here are some starter questions to try:

- ✓ *Where are you from?*
  (Try to find some commonality – If they're from somewhere you are familiar with, identify with them and reflect your knowledge of the place. For example: "Oh! My aunt is from Cleveland, too. I used to visit in the summers... Loved it there!" If it's somewhere you've never been, you can always say, "I've always wanted to go there. I hear it is beautiful.")
- ✓ *Where do you live now?*
- ✓ *Why are you moving?*
- ✓ *How long have you been looking at houses?*
- ✓ *Are you working with a real estate agent now?*
  (We will talk more about this in a minute.)
- ✓ *Have you seen anything you liked?*
- ✓ *When do you need to be in your new home?*
- ✓ *What features of this home worked for you?*
  Or, What features didn't work for you?

From these questions, you can start applying solutions. This is where your original research and market knowledge come into play. Ideally, you can tell them about another house that sounds more suitable to their needs and ask if they would like you to arrange a showing.

The key is to keep them engaged without being pushy. You want to be genuine and conversational. This will work with some, and not with others – some people will just make a beeline for the door and avoid any conversation. That's ok, you can't win everyone over. But follow the suggestions I have laid out or come up with some unique strategies of your own, to set yourself apart, and you will greatly increase your odds of converting your Open House visitors into clients, and ultimately, commissions!

Make sure to give each visitor your business card and do everything you can to get a phone number and/or email address from them. Create a professional, easy-to-read market report about the area, and have it displayed. You can show it to them, then ask them to write down their email address. Let them know that you will happily send them one.

Methods of capturing contact information

Open Home Pro is a great Open House app that allows you to create a quick profile of the property and have guests sign in using an iPad. Some people prefer this over filling out a registration form or signing in on an Open House registry. The benefit to this is that you won't have to struggle to read messy handwriting and try to interpret emails and phone numbers, and the guest will be sent the property information and your contact information.

Some people will download the app, others might enter a drawing, and some may be willing to add their email to a list for market information – if you have all of these options available, you will increase your chances of getting the most information from your visitors.

Follow-up

Later that day (or, at the latest, the following morning), everyone who visited should receive a "Thank you" communication from you. Ideally, it will be a phone call to discuss the next steps. If you don't have their phone number, then your email communication should have a call to action – something to get them to call you.

Agents are often worried about having all the answers. I think that having something to get back to them with is a **great** way to follow up. So, if they ask if they could put up a fence at this house, tell them you want to do some research and get back to them. If you only have their email, then send them an email that says, "I have the answer to your question. Please give me a call at your earliest convenience to discuss." Or, you might say "Hey, I found a great house that I think will be perfect for you. Give me a call ASAP, because it's about to hit the market and won't last long!"

See what I did there? If I just gave them the answer, then there is a good chance I will never hear from them.

Disclaimer: Be sure you actually do have a house in mind to show them. Don't use a "bait and switch" approach!

Long-term follow-up

Each contact from your Open House should be added to your CRM and put on a follow-up plan based on their individual situation. If they are in town visiting family, and are thinking of buying here next year, put them on a long-term campaign, where they receive something of value from you bi-weekly (valuable market information, mortgage tips, etc.). Include quarterly phone calls to check in and see how their plans are going for the move. If they are looking now, then your follow-up plan should be immediate and include sending them properties daily. You know they are online every day looking at homes, the idea is to get them to search using your website. Keep in mind that they could be receiving information from several agents, what are you going to do to stand out from the others?

Do they "really" have an agent already?

This brings me to my comment earlier about asking the question, "Are you currently working with a real estate agent?"

When you first meet someone, their first instinct is to try and blow you off. The easiest way to do this is to tell you they already have an agent. This might be true, and it might be "kind of" true, but you need to get to the bottom of it early on. So, if they say they are working with an agent, ask more questions. Maybe not immediately, but if they continue to engage with you, there are some probing questions you can ask to help uncover if they really have a relationship with someone, or if they were just putting you off.

In some cases, you might ask the name of the agent they are working with. For example, say something like, "Great, do you have their card with you? I'd love to let them know you stopped by." To this, they may produce the information (in which case, you want to respect that relationship and follow up with the agent), or they might say something like, "Well, we have someone sending us properties, but we haven't met them yet."

In that case, I would continue to build rapport with this person until I could uncover the nature of the relationship with the online agent. I would never recommend you try and take over an established relationship – remember the "golden rule" and good old Karma! Treat others as you would like to be treated, right? But, what you do want to find out is if there really is a relationship. Just be your brilliant, genuine and engaging self, and they will start letting you in.

Pro Tip:

> If you are working with buyers, they should always have a stack of your
> business cards *and* be educated about what to do if they stumble upon an
> Open House or a new home community. Often, they honestly don't know
> how it works, and they may not know that if they view a home without
> disclosing your relationship, you might not be able to represent them in
> the purchase. When you explain it to them, make sure you explain the
> benefits for them, not the benefits for you.

Every Day Action Item:

> If you are brand new and haven't done so yet, arrange to visit or shadow
> some experienced agents as they conduct Open Houses. If you have done
> that, then jump in! Schedule Open Houses for the next several weekends
> and follow my suggestions above to optimize the results!

Floor Time

Sometimes also called "up time" or "opportunity time," this is when you are the
agent on duty in your office for a particular period of time. During that time,
any non-represented business that comes in will be your opportunity. Different
offices have varied policies, so I won't get into the details, but it is important
that you are prepared to make the most out of this time.

Here are a few tips to make the most out of your floor time opportunity.

Come with the right mindset. Depending on your location, brokerage and
market, you may have a high level of walk-in and call-in business in your office,
or you might have very little. In either case, you need to prepare yourself mentally. In a busy, high-traffic office, you need to be ready to work.

Have a visual list of questions or talking points in a place where you can easily
access them. These are quick reference interview questions to get to know the
needs of the caller.

Know your market: Be ready with new listings, hot price points, new
construction, and have your MLS system open on your computer. Nothing
is worse than having someone on the phone and asking them to hold on while
you log in – especially if you struggle with passwords or technology in general.

If you are new to your office, be sure you have a clear understanding of how to operate the office phones.

Pro Tip:

>   If you are challenged when it comes to technology, consider having a conversation and gathering all their information and questions first. Tell them you will get right back to them. This might be risky, because some people want immediate gratification and might move on to someone else – but it's better than keeping them on the phone while you fumble with the process.

If you are in a market or office with low traffic, you might have several floor shifts in a row with absolutely no business. This is why you need the right mindset. Is this the most valuable use of your time? When you are new, why not?

You might get some business – just be ready to have other productive work to do during that time. Don't use this as social time to catch up with people in your office or play games on your phone. Have some work lined up that you can do, and if some new business comes in – bonus! But if not, you got work done. Being in the office environment can also be beneficial. Use this time to listen to what is going on around you and absorb the real estate culture.

Every Day Action Item:

Talk to your broker or manager about floor time opportunities in your office and take steps to get on the schedule.

Chapter Twelve: Sphere of Influence & Past Clients – Don't Be A Secret Agent

One of the most important facets of your real estate career is making sure *everyone* knows that you are in the business of helping people buy and sell homes. You cannot keep your business a secret!

"Don't be a secret agent" may bring a few laughs, but I urge you to take it very seriously. Failure to keep in touch with people you know and remind them of your professional value can lead to disappointment. Nothing is worse than discovering that friend or family member just completed a real estate transaction *without you.*

Sphere of Influence

Your sphere of influence (SOI), or "center of influence," as it's sometimes called, is the network of people you influence because you actually know them. These are your family, friends, business relationships and common organization or club members. Statistics show that a great deal of your business will come from this group of people, so it is crucial that you foster and grow these relationships on a regular basis.

You may think to yourself, "I don't know that many people," or "I just moved here, and all of my family and friends are in another state."

I am here to tell you that you know more people than you think, and, the good news is that you can grow your sphere of influence quickly by adding new names to your network every day! Also, you still have opportunities with people who live in another areas through referral business.

The first step in optimizing your SOI is to get them all in one place. No, I don't mean that you have to throw a big party and invite them all over to your house! I am suggesting that you start a database where you can enter and track your activities.

Earlier, I described the benefits of a CRM program. If you have one, great! This is where it comes in handy. If you haven't yet decided on a CRM, then I recommend starting a spreadsheet or document where you can enter and keep this information. The nice thing about a program like Microsoft Excel is that you should be able to import and export information in and out of any program easily from a formatted spreadsheet.

Building Your SOI Database

Now, the big question: "Who do I put into my database?"

The easy answer is: *Everyone you know!*

First: Start with family. It doesn't matter where they live – add them in there.

Then: Move on to friends. Add best friends, good friends, past friends' new friends – it sounds like a Dr. Seuss book! Facebook, Instagram and Twitter can be great resources for this.

Third: Add your neighbors. If your neighborhood has a published directory – bonus! If not, sign up for the NextDoor platform. This platform contains a wealth of information, and many people put their email address and phone numbers in their profile.

Remember, when we talk about SOI, we are talking about people who know you. So, if you haven't met them yet, or they wouldn't know you by name, they aren't ready to have a place in your SOI quite yet. If your neighborhood has planned activities, a community pool or clubhouse, or group yard sales (or anything similar!), attend social events to get to know your neighbors. Make sure you take your business cards with you – ready to distribute them to your new friends if the opportunity presents itself!

Fourth: Include people you have done business with in the past. Not real estate business, because they would likely be categorized as "past clients", but people you have worked with in past jobs or careers. LinkedIn is a good resource for finding these connections.

Finally: Add all the people you interact with on a regular basis during a typical week or month. Your grocery store clerk, mail carrier, hairdresser, insurance agent, financial planner, attorney or bank teller. Consider people you would smile at in passing, even if you don't know their names, like teachers at your kids' school or daycare, other parents on your kids' sports or after-school teams, or people you see frequently at the gym. As you interact with these people, be friendly and conversational. Offer your card and ask for their contact information. At the very least, get their name, so you can send them a friend request on Facebook or connect on LinkedIn, which leads to more familiarity.

As you continue to build your SOI lists, find ways to interact with these people on a regular basis and stay at the "top of mind" for them.

Working Your SOI Database

Here are some tips and guidelines for effectively communicating with your SOI:

Interacting with family

You might think that interacting with your family, is a "no brainer." You may assume that your family knows that you are in real estate, and when they have a need, they will contact you.

Not so fast. If you have close relationships with certain (local) members of your family, then yes, they may be aware of your ability to help them. But anyone outside of your immediate daily contact just might "forget" when the time comes.

In most cases, you can receive a referral fee for referring a family member to a local real estate professional. So, be sure to have regular interaction with your family members near and far, reminding them of what you do.

Nothing is more disappointing than when you get your annual holiday letter from distant relatives and find out they sold their house and moved into a retirement community! If this happens, the only person you can blame is yourself.

They didn't leave you out of the loop on purpose. Chances are good that they simply didn't know that you could benefit from their sale. *Don't be a secret agent!*

How you communicate with your family (near and far) is a very individual thing – and really depends on your relationship with them. Are you friends with them on Facebook? Do you send them cards for birthdays and holidays or write regular letters? Do you call them to check in from time to time? These are all opportunities to remind them that you can help them, or *anyone they know*, with a real estate transaction.

Your friends and family are also your best source of referrals, so even if they don't have an immediate need, chances are they know someone who is getting ready to make a move. Make sure they have a supply of business cards on hand.

Interacting on social media

On social media sites, the key is: *Be yourself.*

Be genuine and helpful. Post interesting photos, articles and statistics that are simple and eye catching. Remember though, people like to be "buyers" – they don't like to be "sold to." Keep your social media feed professional, but casual, and position yourself as a community leader. Don't make all your social media posts about real estate.

As a community leader, show your social media circles that you're "in the know" about events, development and current issues. Review a new restaurant or retail store. Post about new businesses or attractions coming to the area. Congratulate local leaders, artists and businesses for their success, anniversaries or other highlights.

The "word of mouth" impact this has can be enormous. It can take *up to two years* for your followers to see you as a true authority, but they will begin to share, re-post, and tell others what they heard from you. When they talk, they will mention you. This free personal promotion accumulates a snowball effect with consistent, captivating content.

Pro Tip 1:
Post content consistently. The more that people see you post good, relevant information online, the more likely they are to remember you when they have a real estate need.

Pro Tip 2:
Whenever someone provides you a referral, send them a handwritten "Thank you" note with a small gift, such as a box of chocolate-covered strawberries or a small bouquet of flowers.

Whether a referral from a friend, family member or anyone in your larger social circle turns into a transaction, reward their effort. If their referral turns into a closed transaction, then reach out again with another "Thank You." Consider including a larger gift, such as a gift card for a nice restaurant.

Every Day Action Item:

Write five handwritten notes each day, until you have reached out to your entire SOI. Once you have sent a note, set a reminder for the next contact. Be sure to engage with your entire SOI on social media on a regular basis, so you stay at the top of their mind and the top of their newsfeed!

Interacting with Past Clients

As you start to close real estate transactions, it is important that you have a plan in place to keep regular contact with those clients.

Statistics show that people move every 5-7 years. In addition to this, your past clients are also an important source for referral business. If done correctly, once you get started, your business will grow organically from repeat and referral business, so do **not** let these opportunities slip past you.

According to an annual survey conducted by the National Association of Realtors, more than 70% of home buyers and home sellers said they would use their agent again or would refer them to friends. Unfortunately, statistics also show that approximately 70% of consumers had forgotten the name of their agent after the first year. Clearly, it is crucial to the longevity of your business that you find meaningful ways to stay in touch with your clients long after the sale!

Here are five great strategies to consistently nurture your relationship with former clients. Remember – always be genuine and provide consistent value.

One: Immediately place them on an automated campaign in your CRM. This could simply be periodic reminders to call and check in, a holiday email campaign, automated market report or a combination of these things. Remember to always note their birthdays and the anniversary of their home purchase. Be sure to reach out on those milestone dates.

Two: About a week after the closing, call the client to check in. Ask how the move is going, if they are settling in, and if there is anything you can do to assist. Let them know how much you enjoyed working with them and that you will be in touch. This is also a good time to ask them for a review or testimonial. We will talk more about collecting testimonials a little later, but you should be sure to ask for an honest review.

Three: About a month after closing, send a handwritten note with a couple of your business cards. Thank the client again for working with you and ask that they share these cards with anyone they know who might have a real estate need, now or in the future. This is where your personality should shine through – be clever and thoughtful with these periodic communications.

Noting personal things about my clients helped me. I used those details to make my communications more meaningful. One client, for example, had lost their grown daughter in a tragic accident. The wife had a beautiful butterfly pendant that she said was symbolic of her daughter always being with her. She always wore clothing and jewelry with butterflies. After closing, I purchased them a butterfly-themed gift for their house, and when I sent a card, it had a butterfly on it. This meant so much to them, and they used me two years later to purchase an investment condo.

Four: Once or twice per year, provide an unsolicited CMA or Market Report. People are always interested in the market activity in their neighborhood and in the potential value of their home. You never know their current situation, and you may just catch them at a time when they are thinking of making another move. After you send it to them, either by mail or email, be sure to follow up with a phone call to see if they have any questions. This adds to the value and allows you to more thoroughly gauge if they might be thinking about selling.

Five: If the clients work in an office environment, I recommend a quarterly "drop by" with some treats for the office. A box of donuts or maybe a hot pizza. Drop by and say hi, then leave your gift in the office break room for everyone to enjoy. Make sure your branding is visible on the box or package, and people will be talking about it all day.

"Hey, who brought the pizza"?
"Cindy's real estate agent!"
"Really? I bought my house six months ago and never heard from my agent again."

This strategy has added impact, because it not only keeps you top of mind with your past client, but also exposes your greatness to everyone they work with.

Implementing these strategies should be a part of your marketing plan with each and every closed transaction. Consistent, thoughtful and strategic contact with your clients will ensure that they not only remember your name, but that they will also continuously reinforce your value.

Every Day Action Item:

Identify all your past clients who live in a 20-mile radius and find out where they work. Schedule to drop by with goodies for the office. Schedule a drop-by visit quarterly.

EVERY DAY AGENT

Chapter Thirteen: Farming – You Reap What You Sow

Farming

If you aren't familiar with the concept of farming, it is simply focusing your marketing efforts on a specific geographic area or demographic in order to become an expert in that area. The idea here is to become the "go to" agent in a particular market. If you are new to real estate, then getting that initial foothold can be quite challenging. But a little outside-the-box thinking, and your dynamic personality will soon have you become the talk of the town!

First, you must become an expert in the community. Visit every home on the market, research the sales and market trends over the last 1-2 years, and study area demographics. You should know the local schools, the distance to major highways, hospitals, shopping, entertainment, restaurants, or other information a potential buyer might ask for.

Second, set up an MLS search that automatically alerts you of *any* activity in your farm area. If a house goes on the market, goes pending, sells or has a price reduction, you should know about it. When a new house comes on the market, be sure to go and preview the home.

Third, conduct as many Open Houses as you can in that neighborhood and implement successful Open House strategies. Be sure your signage has your name on it, and that you advertise on NextDoor, social media sites and print media. The more people see your name around the neighborhood, the more likely they will be to see you as the neighborhood expert.

Fourth, invest in a quality mailing service that will send out professional marketing pieces to your farm area on a regular basis. This is a softer, more passive approach, but consistency pays off. Even though they are likely to toss the piece in the recycle bin on their way up the driveway, the subliminal message will get through. They will see your name on the marketing piece on a regular basis, establishing your brand recognition. The more useful and relevant the information, the better.

At least one mailing per year should be an item of value that people will keep. In years past, magnetic calendars were an excellent option. However, today, not so much. The days of hanging up a calendar in the kitchen are pretty much a thing of the past. However, a shopping list or note pad would be something that people might be more likely to keep on their counter or throw in a drawer to use on occasion. Once, I informally polled a group of my friends, and they said that chip clips are one of their favorite promotional items to receive. You can never have too many chip clips. Be sure the item is branded with your name, photo and contact information. Another great idea is branded USB flash drives. They can be inexpensive and get a lot of use!

Fifth, not everyone is a fan of the car magnet, but with this tool, you can get a lot of bang for your buck. Have easy-to-read magnets made for both sides of your car. Some people go as far as window decals and even car wraps, but at the very least, magnets do the trick. Make it a point to drive around your farm area on a regular basis. Do it when the weather is nice, during times of the day when people are out walking. Smile and wave at people. Be visible.

Sixth, if the community has any type of regular event, such as an annual barbecue or street party, offer to sponsor the event by providing one major food item, such as the meat course or dessert. If they have a community yard sale event, offer to provide the signage for the event. Be sure to drive around to each house that is participating and talk to the owners. This is an excellent opportunity to find out if anyone is planning to move!

Seventh, instead of conventional door knocking, try door knocking with a purpose. Whenever there is activity in your farm neighborhood, go out and visit 20 or so homes around that activity. This way, when they answer the door, you have a good reason for being there. Let them know that you are keeping an eye on real estate activity and thought they might be interested to know that the home down the street just went on the market or went pending or sold. As you begin to leave, you can pull the old "Columbo" move:

Turn slowly back around and say, "Oh, one more thing... Do you know anyone who might be looking to move to the area or who is thinking about selling?"

Every Day Action item:

Identify one neighborhood of 200-400 homes and become familiar with the inventory. Set up an MLS auto search for immediate updates of all activity and schedule open houses in that neighborhood whenever possible.

Chapter Fourteen: For Sale by Owner – Opportunity Hides in Plain Sight

I can hear the groans now. There is something about the mention of this acronym that causes most real estate agents to run for the hills. It astounds me that more agents don't see the opportunity here. Or, maybe they see it, but they just don't know the right approach.

Homes that are For Sale By Owner (abbreviated "FSBO" and pronounced "Fiz-bow") are, in my opinion, one of the **best** sources of new listing business. They should be a part of your regular prospecting plan. These are people who you know need to sell their home. Agents spend countless hours and thousands of dollars farming and cold calling people at random, but they fail to see the value in approaching people who are attempting to sell their home on their own.

How to Find FSBOs

Many sellers who are attempting to sell on their own do nothing more than put a sign in the yard. It is crucial that you keep an eye out for these opportunities while you are out and about. Take different routes to the places you frequent. Detour down back streets and cruise the neighborhoods in your market area. Some sellers pay a small fee to list their property on Zillow or a FSBO website. You should be looking at these sites daily for new listings as well.

Also, tell people you know to keep an eye out for you. If your friends or family ever see a For Sale by Owner sign, ask them to snap a quick photo and send it to you. Once, I held a "find the FSBO" contest on Facebook. Everyone who sent me a photo of a FSBO was entered in a drawing for a complimentary dinner and a movie.

Why FSBOs fail

The number one thing we know about a FSBO seller is that they don't want to pay commission. They think that by selling their house on their own, they will maximize their profit. Here are some of the main reasons that FSBO sellers may **not** yield the results they are looking for, and the reasons why hiring a professional can net them more money:

One: Correct Pricing

It is likely that the home is not priced correctly. Sellers don't have access to the data needed to accurately price their home, so it could be overpriced. This means it will be overlooked by the people who would be most likely to buy it. Overpriced homes tend to sit on the market for a long time, causing them to become stigmatized, which will eventually drive the price even lower. The home could also be underpriced, causing the homeowner to leave money on the table.

Two: Deal Hunters

People who shop for FSBOs are looking for a deal. They know the seller is not paying commission, and they deduct that from their offer. Effectively, the buyer is saving the commission, not the seller.

Three: Exposure

Someone who is selling a home on their own simply cannot expose the house to enough people. The more people you expose it to, the better the seller's odds of getting top dollar.

Strategies to Build Relationships with FSBOs:

A FSBO seller is generally approached by dozens of real estate agents, but rarely do they ever hear from them again after one or two interactions. They give up. It takes about five interactions with a FSBO seller to earn their business, so keep at it. The reality is that they most likely will not sell the home on their own. Most FSBO sellers give it a try for a while, and then they will list with a professional. If you have been a helpful resource to them, they will likely list with you when they are ready.

First contact

If at all possible, get face-to-face with them. Knock on the door! The objective is to make an appointment to see the house. I recommend using a very non-threatening approach. Let the seller know that you understand they are trying to sell it on their own, and you are **not** there to list it. Tell them that, because this is the area where you work and sell, you make it your business to know all the available inventory. Simply ask if you can see the home. Let them know that you work with many buyers and would be happy to bring any qualified buyers to their home, if they are willing to work with buyers' agents.

Ask questions to establish rapport and uncover their motivation of moving. You can ask where they are going after they sell, or what their timeframe is for moving. Use the motivation that you uncover to your advantage during your subsequent communications. If they say they are moving back up north to be closer to their grandchildren, then you have some prime ammunition when it comes to getting them to list. If you can keep reminding them that those grandbabies are waiting to see their favorite Mimi and Papa, you can point out how you can help them get there faster!

Once you have toured the home, just leave. Don't try to pitch your services. Tell them it was very nice meeting them, make sure they have your card and let them know that you will be looking for a buyer. If you do have a buyer who may be even remotely interested in this home, arrange to show it to them. Be sure you have some sort of written agreement of compensation in place with the seller, prior to showing their home to anyone.

Second contact

Call the FSBO seller a few days after your first meeting to see how things are going. Ask them if they are having a lot of showings and *listen* to their answer. At this point, a general offer of assistance can be made. Just tell them that you understand what they are going through and are happy to answer any questions that may come up. As you interact with them, you can start to plant seeds along the way that illustrate the things they may not know about the home sale process, as well as hint toward the value that you bring to the table.

Prepare a home safety checklist or a home preparation checklist, then you can offer to share these with them. Ask if they understand the state disclosure laws and offer to share a seller's property disclosure questionnaire with them. You are giving them valuable help, while also illustrating that selling their home may not be as easy as they thought!

For sample documents, visit the resource section at EverydayREAgent.com.

Follow-Up

The next three to five contacts are going to depend on the situation, but here are some ideas to help keep the conversation moving forward, as you continue to provide items of value.

One: Open House Help

Offer to hold an Open House for them. Why? Buyers do not like to linger in a house when the seller is present. It is awkward and uncomfortable. Also, you have the resources to promote the Open House to attract more people through advertising and signage, not to mention your ability to reach hundreds of real estate professionals who also have buyers! You are a trained salesperson, and you know how to sell the features of their home and neighborhood.

Two: Professional Promotion

Offer to create a professional flyer for them. Have them send you a few of their favorite photos, and you can create and print some high-quality color flyers for them. Offer it as just a nice perk of knowing you.

Three: Pre-Qualifications

Offer your list of preferred mortgage professionals. Stress how important it is to know that the buyers who come through their house are pre-qualified. Let them know that you always qualify buyers before showing them a home.

Four: Pre-Listing Home Inspection

Ask if they have done a pre-listing home inspection. This can ensure the home is in tip-top shape, and there won't be any issues when the buyer performs their inspection.

Five: Home Warranty

Ask if they have access to a home warranty product. This can be a great marketing tool to provide peace of mind to potential buyers.

As you begin to uncover the seller's motivation and have nurtured the relationship with them along the way, you will be setting the stage for taking over the listing. If you haven't already, ask them how long they intend to try it on their own, before they list with a professional. Set up your follow-up accordingly. Be sure that you are the first person they think of when that time comes!

Every Day Action Item:

Make first contact with five new FSBOs every week and implement a follow-up system as part of your business plan.

EVERY DAY AGENT

Chapter Fifteen: Expired Listings – Mystery Solved!

Expired listings are another great source of listing business, because you know that people whose home listings have expired are people who *need* to sell their home. However, they are usually pretty frustrated with the process and can be a little more challenging. There are several reasons that their home didn't sell, and it's your job to find the issues and apply solutions.

What you will find most often is that the home is overpriced – but don't jump immediately to that conclusion!

For Example:
> Maybe the property has a fenced yard, but online, that feature is not listed. A consumer or realtor who is filtering their property search to specifically only look at properties with a fenced yard would miss this house in their search, if the field for this detail was left blank.

Approach with Caution and Understanding

Here is my process for approaching a seller with a listing that recently expired:

Prior to making first contact, do some research. Study the MLS listing sheet and find the holes in the property's marketing.

The first thing I look at is the photos. For someone looking at the property online, what first impression will they get of the home? If the photos are not professional, it is the perfect talking point to differentiate your services from that of their previous agent. Be sure not to throw the other agent under the bus, simply point out the things you would do differently.

Then, I read the property description and look for key features of the property that the other agent missed, such as the example above where the house's fenced yard was not highlighted for online search.

I recommend contacting the seller the day that the listing expires, if possible. You can send a simple message that says something like, "I understand your home is no longer being marketed in MLS. Do you still want to sell it?"

If the owner still wants to sell

If the seller responds to say "Yes!" then you can follow up by saying: "I specialize in selling homes other people couldn't sell."

There are many ways a seller can respond to this. They may want to know why they haven't met you before. I've even had sellers ask me, "Why didn't you show the house when it was listed?"

In this case, I sometimes take the approach to tell the homeowner that I "work with more sellers than buyers," and again, emphasize that I specialize in working with sellers whose homes didn't sell during its first listing. Often, I tell the homeowner, "I think it's important to focus on why it didn't sell and discuss new strategies your previous agent may not have considered." This approach – letting them know you're bringing something new to the table – can be enough to get them interested to meet with you.

However, if you don't want to give the impression that you largely work only with sellers, and the seller asks, "Why didn't you show my home when it was listed?" it can often be helpful to take the approach of: "You know, I was wondering why it didn't show up on my radar. I'd like to meet with you and find out why that happened."

You can still let the seller know that you work with both buyers and sellers, and that you're interested in helping them solve whatever problem has been causing their home sale to stall.

When you tell a homeowner whose listing has expired that you want to find out "what went wrong," they may be defensive or discouraged. Often, homeowners in this situation will ask me, "Oh yeah? How are you going to do things differently?"

The best thing to do is meet with them face-to-face. Don't try to sell yourself and your skills over the phone or via email. If they are hesitant, you don't have to be pushy. Simply use your charm and expertise to set up an appointment at their earliest convenience:

> *"I'd be glad to discuss my approaches with you. Thanks for asking what makes me different from your previous agent! When is a good time for us to meet? I'd love to see the house in person and discuss my strategies with you."*

If the owner says "No, I'm taking my house off the market."

If the owner says they are no longer interested in selling their house, ask them: "If I were to bring you a qualified buyer *today* – a buyer who wanted to pay a fair price for your home and close within your time frame – would you want me to sell it?"

Again, the seller may respond in a number of different ways.

If they ask, "Do you have that buyer?" turn it around and let them know you have several buyers interested and pre-qualified, but you're not sure if you have the right one for them, because you haven't seen their house yet. Then, try to schedule an appointment to meet with them.

They may say, "No. We're going to take a break. We're not interested in selling it now." If this is the case, be empathetic and helpful:

> *"You must be tired of everything that goes with having your house for sale. I totally understand. Since you already invested the time to get your house ready, wouldn't it make sense to get you that quick offer, so you can move on? I'd love to discuss this in person."*

But, if the seller simply says, "Yes! I would sell if you brought me that buyer today," then you're on your way! Jump on the chance and ask them when their schedule is open to meet with you – hopefully in the next day or two.

If the seller opens up and "dumps" all of their experience and frustrations on you – **listen**. Empathize and ask questions:

- ✓ Why do you think it didn't sell?
- ✓ Did your agent conduct Open Houses or broker tours?
- ✓ Did you try enhanced internet marketing or targeted social media marketing?
- ✓ Did your last agent complete a salability checklist?

Often, you will spark the seller's interest and prompt them to ask you questions about your process. With the mention of a "salability checklist" or enhanced marketing techniques, don't be surprised if the seller responds, "I don't know about that. What is it?" This is your opportunity to shine!

Describe anything they're not familiar with and explain how your process is different from other agents. One successful approach is to explain that your tools – such as checklists and targeted online marketing – are unique and customized for your clients. Emphasize how you have developed your own techniques that result in success for your clients. Then, explain that you'll be happy to share your proven approaches with them, during a face-to-face meeting.

The objective is to **get the appointment**, not to solve their problems and concerns on the phone.

Accepting their "No"

If the homeowner still says, "No," that's okay.

Ask them: "Would it be okay to keep in touch with you over the next couple of months, in case anything changes? May I send you information on market activity in your area?"

With their permission, stay in touch with them. They may just be burned out and need some time to prepare themselves to try again. Be there for them when they are ready.

Of course, if you are working with a buyer who might be interested in their home, ask them if you can show it. When they see that you are working for them, even without the formal listing agreement, they will certainly think of you when they are ready to list again.

Regardless whether they list their property with you, be sure to have a written commission agreement in place before showing the property to any potential buyers.

Every Day Action Item:

Set up MLS to notify you of all expired listings in your market area (filtered by zip code, county, city, neighborhood, etc.). Every morning, research all expired listings and make the first contact (a call or visit), as soon as possible.

PART FOUR – REALTOR FOR LIFE

Chapter Sixteen: Customer Service – Go the Extra Mile. It's Never Crowded

When I work with my clients, buyers and sellers, they know from the start that I have their best interest in mind. The word people use to describe me more often than any other is "genuine." I truly care about my clients. I care about their specific needs, helping to protect them and their greatest asset. I care about their experience from start to finish.

You will need to develop your unique style, but I am going to share with you some things I have done to set myself apart and become the "realtor for life" to my clients.

Humor

I have found that almost all my initial interactions with people start with some level of humor. It cuts the tension and puts everyone at ease. Whether it's a reference to the weather or a crack about the absurdity of a situation, a well-crafted "funny" breaks through an uncomfortable situation.

For Example:
When I knock on the door of an expired listing, I usually open the conversation with a joke, something like, "I bet I'm the first real estate agent you've seen all day." Most likely, they have been approached by many – so, it's funny and sometimes gets them to let their guard down.

Always remember: *It's about them, not you.*

As real estate professionals, we want to sell ourselves to people that we meet by "feature dumping" on them. Stop it. Ask questions and get to know them and their individual needs. You will demonstrate your value organically through your actions and responses.

As you get to know them, note personal details such as their birthday, anniversary, where their parents or children live, pets, hobbies and interests. Write these down and refer to them as you move through the process. You will also use this information for long-term follow-up.

Be Responsive

You can't always be available to answer texts, emails and phone calls immediately, but in order to establish yourself as a valuable resource, you need to respond within a reasonable timeframe. I receive this feedback from my clients frequently. They rave about how quickly I respond when they have a question or a need. Many have commented to me that I "always" answer their calls, even when I know I haven't.

*Being attentive and responsive makes **every** client feel like they are your **only** client.*

I might be frantic and overwhelmed on the other end, but I always stop and respond to the needs of my client, without making them feel they are interrupting. Stop. Take a breath. Smile when you answer the phone.

Be cognizant of how people read your text or email messages. Before you send them, **stop and re-read them**. Make sure your message is clear and can't be misinterpreted. Use emoticons to add a little wink or smile at the end to remind them of the friendly tone of your voice. You want to consistently remind them that you're a professional and pleasant to do business with.

Going "Above and Beyond" with Buyers

When working with buyers, I work to make their experience as special and *stress free* as possible. Most of this "special" experience is in the preparation and execution of showing them the properties. In property tours, there are a lot of moving parts. You need to be on top of the details and plan for anomalies.

Educating buyers

Educating buyers on the process is key to a successful relationship. It is important for them to know what to expect throughout the many steps in the process, so you can prevent potential distractions that cause them to purchase a home without you. You want them to know what they can expect from you, that you will work with them *as long as it takes* to find the right home. Once they find the home, you will use your expert negotiation skills to get them the best deal and protect their best interest. You will help them navigate through the complicated "contract to closing" process by recommending service providers, attending inspections, working with the lender and handling communication with the other parties involved. You provide them an excellent value.

All your clients should be given a stack of your business cards and told that if they visit an Open House, builder model or see any property that catches their interest, they should call you prior to speaking with anyone else – no other agents, or contractor salespeople. They shouldn't speak with anyone without contacting you first. Let them know that if they initiate a contact with another realtor, you may not be able to provide your expertise and assist them in the rest of the process – and they'd really be missing out!

If they do give in to the temptation of an open house or builder model, and you are not with them, tell them to give the other agent one of your cards. They should let the other agent or salesperson know that they already have an agent. This establishes an exclusive relationship, letting the buyer know that you will be their one-and-only real estate agent through the process.

When a buyer does stray, it often isn't on purpose. Some consumers simply don't know how it works. Real estate transactions often work differently in different areas, so consumers need to be educated on the process for the area where they are looking to buy.

> **Did you know:** In the U.K., a consumer can only buy a house from the "Estate Agent" who listed the house? There are no buyers' agents. If you are working with someone from the U.K., they might be calling every listing agent to see different homes, because they don't know they can work with a buyer's agent.

Buyer representation and buyer broker agreements

What about buyer representation agreements or buyer broker agreements? Well, there are varying rules and opinions on these, and I defer to your broker on this subject.

As a general rule, I did not use them, except for rare and exceptional situations. I believe that an agent can earn a buyer's loyalty easily by both educating them and offering "above and beyond" service.

There may be some clients who you determine are a "flight risk," based on a lack of emotion (like an investor or corporate client), a lack of knowledge of how our buyer relationships work, or any other factor that sets off your "sixth sense." If something is telling you that you might have difficulty establishing loyalty with a client, then by all means, introduce a buyer agreement that puts their obligations in writing.

Mortgage pre-qualification

Help buyers establish their financial situation. Assist them with mortgage pre-qualification, if they are getting a loan to purchase the property. Always have this conversation prior to showing them houses, and always offer them more than one option.

As you close more transactions, you will establish relationships and loyalty to specific lenders. Be careful to offer your client options. If something goes wrong, you don't want the client to claim that you "told them" to use a specific lender. Give them two or three choices of great lenders you have relationships with, then your clients can select. The ultimate choice is on them.

When you first approach the subject, don't say you "won't show them houses" until you verify that they are qualified. Ouch! Instead, let them know that it's best to understand their complete financial picture to ensure that:

1) You are definitely looking at homes in the right price point.
2) When you and the buyers find the right home, you can structure an offer immediately.

Make sure you clearly show them that the benefit of pre-qualification is for *them*, not you.

Searching for homes

Once I ask all the necessary questions to uncover their needs, I start the search for homes. I start with a broad search and send them the results, along with a note saying that I always start the search with wider parameters, and as they give feedback, I will narrow the search.

For Example:

If your buyers reject homes, saying the houses are "too close together," try focusing on homes with larger lots.

There is a real estate industry saying that: "Buyers are liars."

While I feel the wording is a little harsh and misleading, I agree with the general premise.

Sometimes, buyers say they will not buy a house in a neighborhood with an HOA, but once they see options in non-HOA neighborhoods, they change their mind. They weren't exactly *lying*, but they didn't know the options. Things change. People change their minds. You have to think outside the box and stretch the options to include all the possible properties.

Touring the Homes

After you narrow down the options, you are ready to schedule tours. How many homes you see in one day depends on your buyers' timeframe. I once showed 15 houses in one day in a 50-mile area. I would **never** recommend this, but these folks were relocating and only had one home-finding day. I planned out the day as efficiently as possible, and we ultimately found them a house – less than 10 minutes from my office. (Go figure!) Of course, this is the exception. Most people are not on a tight schedule like that.

Customize your tour schedule based on their needs and be as efficient as possible with the time allotted.

The logistics

When scheduling each showing, leave time for travel. Overlap the appointments to allow for lag time. You never know how long the buyer might spend in each house. They may walk into a house and immediately dismiss it, so a showing you allowed 30 minutes for, only took 10 minutes. Conversely, a buyer may linger in a home for an hour. This is a good sign, of course, but it can also throw off a tight showing schedule.

I map out the properties in a logical driving order, then overlap as follows:

> If I am showing the first house at 10 a.m., I make the showing window from 10-11 a.m. Then, the second house I schedule between 10:30-11:30 a.m., and so on.

This is assuming that there is only a 5 to 10-minute drive between homes. If the drive is longer, you need to allow more time for that.

Property details

Prepare a folder or clipboard for the buyers with a print-out of each property that they will see, in the order they will see them. I always drive and have the buyers in the car with me, whenever possible. Then, on the way to a house, they can look over the details, and I can "Wow" them with my knowledge of the home and community.

Transition from one location to the next by saying things like, "I'm really excited to show you the next house. It is only two blocks from the school you wanted and has a big, fenced backyard for Scooter. And, it has that private office you were looking for, Scott!" Make it personal and show them that you did your research.

Then, after the showing, we talk about the house. I have them rate it. You can use a scale from 1 through 5, or have them grade it A, B, C, D, F – like in school. This helps the buyers sort out what they really liked, so you know which ones might need to be revisited and which can be eliminated.

Also, if you tour several houses in one day, it's fun to give them each a nickname that reflects its most memorable feature. You might call one the "pink bedroom house," and another the "tropical oasis house." When you refer to the houses that way, buyers immediately recall which house you are talking about. Because, believe me, several houses run together by the end of the day. Encourage your buyers to take notes on the property information sheet that you provided.

The practicalities

Think about the comfort and convenience of your clients during the tour. If you and they will be in the car all day, pack bottled water and a variety of snacks. If time allows, schedule a lunch break and take them somewhere nice in the community where they want to live.

Always consider bathroom breaks and discourage your buyers from using the bathrooms in the homes you view. As you can imagine, a lot can go wrong. Keep toilet paper, a towel, baby wipes and hand sanitizer in your car, just in case of an emergency, and *always* check to be sure the water is on in the house, before giving them the "go ahead."

However, it's best to schedule stops to allow buyers to "take care of business" along the way. Every two or three homes, ask loudly in the car, "Does anyone need a bathroom break?" and wait until everyone has answered before setting off for your next destination. Don't wait for an emergency. Trust me, your buyers will appreciate that you are being thoughtful of their needs.

Professional communications during tours

As a courtesy to sellers and your fellow real estate professionals, if you are running early or late by more than 10 minutes, call the listing agent, so they can inform the sellers. This is common courtesy and ensures a more comfortable showing experience for everyone.

In my opinion, it's simply rude when the person I'm with is on the phone constantly, or if their phone is frequently ringing and dinging. When with clients, showing property or otherwise, it's good practice to put your phone on silent. Use your auto-text feature to tell callers you will get back to them.

You can return urgent calls in moments when your client is occupied – if they are lingering in a house that they like, maybe standing in the kitchen talking about it among themselves, or perhaps they are conversing out by the pool, then you can excuse yourself to quickly call back the other person. Make it quick and only do this when the call is urgent – most calls can wait until you are done with your current client.

Oh – and don't rely solely on your car or phone's GPS. If you aren't 100% certain where you are going, scope it out in advance. GPS systems can take you to unmanned gates, they may not recognize newer roads, or they may take you out of the way to avoid tolls when the direct route was preferred. Don't risk it – do your homework.

Short-notice showings happen

Not all showings will be a full day of touring homes. Sometimes, a client will call and want to run out to see one house immediately. This does not allow you the same amount of time for preparation and scheduling, but you can still be mindful of the experience and help things run as smoothly as possible.

These are things your clients will remember and appreciate. Go above and beyond, and your clients will have a pleasant, easy experience with you. After meeting with you, people will talk about their experience with friends and family, whether it was good or bad. Think about how you want them to talk about you: Do you want them to say you were scattered, disorganized and on the phone the whole time? Or do you want them to say you were thoughtful, attentive and organized?

Every Day Action Item:

Stock up your car with some comfort and necessity items, so you are always prepared for showings!

Going "Above and Beyond" with Sellers

Many of the same common courtesy principles apply when you meet with sellers. Do your homework and be prepared, so they see you as a professional who takes the sale of their home seriously. It's important for the seller to see that you are not there simply because you want a listing – you are there to help them sell their home.

The best thing you can do when working with sellers is *ask a lot of questions*. Then, *really listen* to their answers. They have specific fears and concerns, and you need to hear them. Then, apply solutions to put them at ease. Be honest and genuine in your responses.

House condition

It is very difficult to tell people negative things about their home. However, it is your job. They hire you to sell their home, and you bring your knowledge and experience to the table to get that done. If the house is generally dirty, messy or cluttered, consider giving them a pre-written list of preparations that are suggested they complete before scheduling photography. This way, you aren't pointing out their issues, but showing them the industry's "best practices," and what they can do for maximum results.

For a sample Home Preparation Checklist, visit the resources section at www.everydayreagent.com.

Staging for showings

If you feel the house can benefit from staging, have a third-party resource provide the feedback. Instead of you telling them they have terrible design skills, bring in a professional stager who knows how to broach this subject tactfully, and who can get things in tip-top shape for photos and showings. The seller will appreciate that you provided this added service.

Whether you pay for a professional stager as a part of your "added value service" is up to you, but it should be a resource that you offer when needed.

Price & flexibility

You absolutely must be honest with your sellers when it comes to pricing their home. Too many real estate professionals tell sellers what they want to hear simply to get the listing, and then they hope the seller agrees to price reductions in order to get the home sold.

If you do this, you are doing a disservice to your client and to yourself. Here's why:

If you do the research, you will see that homes that stay on the market longer sell for less than homes that were priced correctly from the start. You can do the research in your individual market to have these statistics ready when you have a discussion about pricing with your sellers.

Stay competitive

Let's say the seller is convinced that their house is worth $350,000, but the comparative market analysis (CMA) shows the market value of the house to be $320,000.

If you list the house for $350,000, you will lose all the buyers who would be willing to pay fair market value of $320,000. Those buyers are searching for homes up to $325,000 or $330,000, and they won't even see the homes listed for $350,000.

After a few months, you finally convince the seller to lower the price. They come down to $340,000, which still isn't in the range for a serious potential buyer to see it. Now, maybe after 90+ days, the seller is upset and challenging your marketing efforts. You convince them to come down to $330,000, and the house sells for $320,000. This is a 92% list-to-sale price ratio.

If your statistics show that homes priced at market value sell for 98% of list price, and you had listed it for $330,000 in the first place, it would have sold immediately for about $325,000. The seller would have gotten more for the house and would have saved three months' worth of carrying costs on the property. Most importantly, they would have been able to move on to their next plan, whatever it was.

Motivate your seller

Discover the seller's motivation and speak to that end. Maybe the seller found another home that they want – perhaps they are selling their starter home for their "forever home," or they are "empty nesters" and ready to downsize. Maybe they are moving to be closer to a new grandchild. Whatever the motivation, speak to it. Tell them you can help them be in their new home, holding that grandbaby, in 30 days!

Protect your stats

There is an added importance to these list-to-sale price ratios. These numbers become your stats. If you can walk into a listing appointment against a competitor and compare your numbers, how do you stack up? You want to be able to say: "My average list-price to sale-price ratio is 98%, and the average time my listings spend on the market is 35 days." Then, you can compare your numbers to the competitor, or to the market in general, and show them that you will get more for their house than other agents!

You need to protect your stats by not taking overpriced listings.

The best tool in your toolbox that will allow you to walk away from an unreasonable seller and an overpriced listing is *more appointments*!

If this one listing is the only opportunity you have going, chances are, you will hold onto it and cave into their price, simply so you have a listing. But, if you have three more appointments later in the week, you can confidently walk away from this listing, knowing there are more opportunities that you can actually sell!

Polished, professional preparation

Follow this guideline to save yourself and your sellers time, money and frustration. Be seen as a competent, knowledgeable professional in the industry.

Once you have the listing, use your listing checklist to be sure you don't miss any details when preparing the home to go on the market. If you have to return to the home several times because you forgot something, you will not look like a seasoned professional. Talk your sellers through the next steps of the process and set up expectations for what they need to do. At the same time, let them know what you will be doing.

For a sample Listing Checklist, visit the resource section at EverydayREAgent.com.

For Example:

You may tell the sellers, "I am going to walk around with my cell phone and take several photos of every room. Don't worry – these are not the photos for marketing. They're just to help me remember the features of each room. I will schedule professional photography for next Thursday. Please follow the home preparation checklist I provided to ensure the best results for the photos. I also need to take measurements of the rooms, unless you have a floor plan from when the home was built?"

Pro Tip:

Call your photographer prior to your appointment and ask them to pencil in their next available time slot. Your sellers will be impressed when you are prepared with a date and time for the photos. You can also list the home quickly, because you already have that in place.

Your pre-sale preparation checklist also includes items such as:

- ✓ Obtaining surveys
- ✓ Reviewing title insurance documents
- ✓ Reviewing HOA or condo documents
- ✓ Gaining access, including keys and alarm code information

Ask sellers to fill out a short property FAQ that you can provide to potential buyers. This FAQ helps answer buyers' common questions about the house. The message you send your sellers here is that you go the extra mile to make it as easy as possible for a buyer to buy their home.

For a sample FAQ, visit the resource section at EverydayREAgent.com.

The Showing Process

You need to discuss the showing process with sellers. Ask how they want appointments to be scheduled and how they want showings to be handled. Strike a balance between honoring their wishes and accommodating the maximum number of buyers.

Some sellers might say they want a 24-hour notice and insist that the listing agent be present at all showings. Tell them the pros and cons of this arrangement, and ultimately let them decide. Be sure they know that the more inconvenient it is to show their property, the fewer people will come to see it.

Ask questions to get to the bottom of why they are making this request. They may simply think it's customary to handle showings this way, and, once you explain that buyers are often crunched for time or may come across their home at the last minute, they might understand the need to be accommodating. Explain that the buyer will be accompanied by a licensed real estate professional, which may put their mind at ease when you can't attend every showing.

Get to the bottom of their concerns. Find a middle ground that keeps them comfortable and allows the most exposure to the home.

Build your property profile

Now, put all your preparation into action. Assemble a binder with all the information on the home, including required disclosures, Homeowner or Condo Association information, a home feature sheet, FAQ sheet, and any other information that helps a buyer decide to buy the home.

Create a high-quality professional flyer for potential home buyers to take with them. Be sure there is always a supply of these flyers, and if you make any changes to the listing (such as a price adjustment), remember to update the flyers and information in the binder.

Once the home is on the market, communication with the seller is essential. Set an expectation with your seller as to how you will communicate with them, and how you would like them to communicate with you. A planned, weekly phone call is usually sufficient. Some sellers are more "hands-on" (in another word, *needy*) and require more frequent communication. If this is the case, tell them to expect a call more often. Choose a day and time (such as "Monday morning" or "Thursday afternoon") and specify that you will update them on the showings for the week, provide them with feedback if there is any, and be ready to discuss Open House activity, at that time.

If you are advertising online, provide statistical data about the effectiveness of the advertising. Remember the promises you made in the beginning and illustrate how you are living up to those promises. Provide results. Discuss strategies to move forward and set future expectations.

My 10/10 rule

*If you have a listing that sits for **10 days with no showings**, or a listing that gets **10 showings with no offers**, you need to adjust your strategy.*

Let the seller know in advance that this is your approach, then follow through.

You and your clients are a team

Selling a home can be very stressful for people. You need to be your sellers' professional advisor, as well as their emotional support throughout the process. Show them you are there for them, doing everything you can to get the best results. Let them know what is happening and what to expect, every step of the way. Set up communication lines, so everyone is on the same page. Work as a team.

Every Day Action Item:

Put together a sample property binder to show at your listing presentations. Show how you go above and beyond to sell their home!

The Transaction

Whether working with a buyer or a seller, once the home goes under contract, be sure that you don't lose focus on the transaction. The work is not done, yet! Be their advocate during negotiation, then oversee the process "from contract to closing." Stay on top of key dates (remember the key dates emails and check-lists from "Chapter Ten: Process Management – Get Your Ducks in a Row"?) and keep open communication with the other agent.

Attend all inspections and keep your buyer or seller on track with their obligations throughout the process. From inspections to appraisals to turning over keys and transferring utilities. Remember, we may do this every day, but they don't.

There are a few points in the transaction that are likely to cause small bumps in the road. Inspections are the most common stress points in the contract-to-close process. Again, whether you are representing the buyer or the seller, talk them through what to expect, so there are no surprises. Make sure all parties understand that the inspector's job is to point out every defect, but that not everything is cause for alarm.

Don't let your emotions or the emotions of the other agent derail the transaction. If you represent the buyer and convey a request for repairs, be sure your request is in writing, supported by documentation, which will usually be the summary sheet of the inspection report. However, *how* you convey your request is vital to the outcome.

Consider these two scenarios:

> You are the listing agent. After the inspection, the buyer's agent calls you and sounds aggravated. They say: "That air conditioner is like a dinosaur and could die at any time. My buyer isn't buying a house knowing that the A/C system is at the end of its life!"

Or,

> You are the listing agent, and after the inspection, the buyer's agent calls you and says: "I'm sending you an email with the inspection summary. Everything went really well, but my buyers are concerned about the age of the air conditioner. We'd like to have an A/C specialist come out and do a further inspection".

Which one of these scenarios will have the better outcome? In the first scenario, the emotion likely comes from the agent, not the buyer. Unfortunately, agents can get caught up with their own needs and forget the needs of the buyer and seller. They may be worried about the deal falling apart because of an old A/C system, and they begin to speak out of fear of not getting a commission check they are counting on.

The truth is, their emotional reaction could cause the deal to fail. I see this frequently. While I understand where the emotion comes from, train yourself to stick with the facts and deal with what is in front of you. You aren't going to get 100% of your deals to the closing table, and if there truly is an issue with the A/C system, you want your buyer to know; you want them to do their due diligence.

We are facilitators of real estate transactions and should always act accordingly. Help your client understand their options and let them make their choices. Then, work professionally with the other agent to bring the parties together. If the other agent is being unprofessional, then you need to be the voice of reason. Bring the transaction back into control, rather than allowing it to become a power struggle between two agents.

Always keep the client's experience in mind. Planning, preparation and a genuine desire to bring all parties together ultimately results in a successful transaction and happy clients all around.

This is how you become your clients' "Realtor for Life!"

EVERY DAY AGENT

Chapter Seventeen: Value Proposition – What Makes You So Special

Your unique value proposition simply and clearly conveys why someone would choose to work with you. It is your "30-second commercial."

To formulate your value proposition, consider these questions:

Who is your niche market?
When you are starting out, you may not have a clearly defined niche, yet. But don't worry, you will find where your talent and passion lie, and they will lead you. Do you primarily work with buyers or do you prefer to be a listing agent? Do you want to be the "expert" of one neighborhood? Do you want to sell to empty nesters or Millennials? Perhaps you want to break into the luxury property market. Once you find your passion, you can define your target audience.

What sets you apart from other agents? How do you go "above and beyond"?
Some things that set you apart might be related to your affiliated brokerage, such as a big brand name with vast exposure, or a local company who has taken over market share in a specific area. Perhaps you have specialized knowledge of distressed properties and the benefits and challenges of these transactions. You might work exclusively with first-time home buyers and have an extensive knowledge of the best financing options and programs that benefit them.

What are your unique qualities?
There are thousands of real estate agents out there, but what sets you apart from the pack? Is it your dedication to the client experience and customer service? Maybe you have a legal or finance background that brings valuable knowledge to the table. Perhaps you have lived in your market area your whole life and have a vast network of colleagues and resources.

What is the one service that you do better than anything else?
Perhaps it's marketing. Maybe you found a way to use video that has generated impressive results. Maybe you are a listing agent with a proven track record of selling homes fast. Have you helped people navigate through the process of purchasing new construction? Do you know the ins and outs of that complicated series of steps?

Put together your answers to formulate your 30-second value proposition speech. You need to convey in a few practiced, measured sentences what makes you valuable.

When you meet someone who asks what you do for a living, consider how to give them an answer that demonstrates what you give your clients – what you do for *them* – rather than simply "what you do" in general.

Rather than saying, "I am a real estate agent," be more specific. Say, "I'm a buyer's agent, and I just love working with first-time homeowners. Know anyone looking to buy for the first time or ready to sell to an eager buyer?" or, "I specialize in selling homes in the downtown neighborhoods, especially from A Street to L Ave. Do you know anyone in that area looking to sell?"

With an answer like this, you have addressed what type of real estate agent you are, and you have given them a little "Wow factor," by showing them that you're professional and passionate.

Try a few different value propositions to see what works for you. Some examples might include:

> "I created a real estate program that makes selling a home as painless and stress free as possible. My marketing – both print and digital – offers sellers maximum exposure and proven results. Are you looking to sell?"

> "Well, I'm proud to say, I can sell a home within 45 days, at or above asking price 95% of the time. I love selling homes in the uptown area, especially between A Street and L Ave. Are you interested in those neighborhoods?"

Even if you are new to the business, you have something to offer clients. Maybe it is something as simple as a promise to return calls within 30 minutes, or maybe it's your persistent dedication to finding them the home of their dreams.

Every Day Action Item:

On a blank sheet of paper, draw one line vertically down the middle, then draw one line horizontally across the middle. You will have four sections.

Label the four sections:
- ✓ My Experience
- ✓ My Qualities
- ✓ My Brokerage
- ✓ My Target Client

Fill each box with words or phrases that pertain to you. Don't think too much, just let your thoughts flow onto the paper.

Some examples can include:

- ✓ Honest
- ✓ Trustworthy
- ✓ Dedicated
- ✓ Resourceful
- ✓ Long-time local
- ✓ Financial background

Keep going until you can't think of anything else. Then, you might set it aside and come back to it an hour later and fill up the rest of the space, as much as you can. When you are done, circle the words that mean the most to you and formulate your 30-second commercial (value proposition).

Chapter Eighteen: Referrals – It's Not Who You Know, It's Who Knows You

I could have added this to Chapter Eleven, where we talked about "spinning plates," because referral business is something you should work on consistently. In the beginning, it is difficult to obtain referrals, but as you close transactions, referrals come faster than you can imagine.

Story from an Every Day Agent: My First FSBO Conversion

Let me tell you about my first FSBO conversion. I was driving through my farm area, taking a different road than normal, and I saw a FSBO sign in a yard. I stopped, knocked on the door – which opened only the slightest crack. I introduced myself, explaining that I was a realtor in the area, specializing in his neighborhood. I asked if I could make an appointment to come back and see the house, in case I had an interested buyer.

He said, "Maybe another time," and I slipped my packet of information through the door, just before it closed.

As I was driving away, my phone rang. It was the seller asking if I could come back. Of course, I did, and I had a lovely meeting with him and his wife. I listed the house. He had been trying to sell it on his own for several months, but in only two days on the market, we got an offer! There were other interested buyers, and I recommended they consider accepting a back-up offer. As it turned out, that was a great idea, because the first buyer backed out before the inspections.

The second offer went through to sell the house without a hitch, and this couple was beyond thrilled. I implemented all the customer service techniques that I suggest in this book, and they raved about their experience. The best part? Well, he was "that guy" in the neighborhood. He was the guy who knew everyone. He took care of things – he changed people's light bulbs and brought in their newspapers. He was the HOA president, and he knew *everyone*.

Not long after his home closed, they moved off to another area closer to family. One day, he called me, saying that his friend down the street from his previous house wanted to sell. That was the most expensive house on the street, and it was my next listing. That was also a fun story. I had a broker Open House and invited my office for lunch to view the house. During the broker open, a random passerby saw the signs and asked if they could see the house. It was exactly what they were looking for, and they bought it! Then, the seller of that house referred a friend from his Rotary Club to me. He was selling his house in another neighborhood and moving back to Germany ... the chain of referrals goes on and on.

I will also tell you: At the time this happened, I was struggling. I had been working FSBO and expired listings, but I was having a hard time getting anything to stick. As soon as this happened, the gates opened. I marketed those listings, which lead to more listings. I had open houses that led to buyer leads. Business led to more business.

The best way to optimize this is to be the **best** at what you do. Always go the extra mile. Be genuine. Protect your clients by looking after their best interest – *not yours*.

Your clients will become raving fans. They will tell their friends, neighbors, co-workers and family about their experience. You will be their Realtor for Life!

Referrals, Revisited

Refer back (*haha!* Get it?) to our discussion about your "Sphere of Influence, where I shared some of my strategies about referrals. Seriously though, referrals should be an integral part of your prospecting.

Office or home drop-by visits and keeping in touch with past clients are basic. On top of being in the habit, remember: When you reach out, ask for referrals. Make sure you end every communication – whether it's a text, email or phone call – by asking the other person for referrals.

I'm not talking about having it in your email signature or printed on the back of your business cards. You've seen this phrase before, right?: "The best compliment you can give me is to pass my name to friends and family."

I hate to break this to you, but *nobody* is reading that!

When you make periodic connections with people, you need to say, "I really enjoyed working with you, and I'm glad we sold your home so quickly. How is everything in your new place?"

At some point in the conversation, they will say how grateful they are or what a great job you did.

Then, you reply, "Thank you! It was my pleasure. Of all the people you know, who can benefit from my great service? Do you know anyone thinking of moving?"

Or at the end of your conversation, if it didn't come up, say, "Don't forget to tell your friends what a great job I did – I'm never too busy to help more people."

You have to be you. Authentic. Use your personal style but **ask**.

Testimonials

I cannot conclude this chapter without talking about testimonials. Today, testimonials are more important than ever. No matter how someone heard about you, they **will** *search your name online before they meet you.*

With the technology of today, first impressions are rarely made face-to-face. People "Google" other people, before even giving them an in-person chance. It's always safe to assume that when you meet someone face-to-face, they already have an impression of you from what they read online.

If they search for you online, what are they going to find? Have you Googled yourself? Do that now and see how you come across on the world wide web. If you're making a poor impression online, you won't even get to the point of meeting with clients face-to-face. If they see unprofessional pictures, negative reviews and a poor representation of your business online, they will turn and head for the hills before you ever get a chance to meet them.

If you search yourself online and you find you have a negative reputation, consider looking into the services of a *reputation management company*. They will help you assess how to best boost your online reputation. Once they get it cleaned up, you should be able to maintain a glowing reputation online by collecting your own testimonials and monitoring your branded online content.

Have one online testimonial portal

You should have *one* general location for collecting client testimonials. Collect all your testimonials on your personal website, Zillow, Yelp or whatever platform works for you. The idea is that when someone asks you for "references" or if they Google you to see what previous clients have said, they will land in one central location, where they can find out a lot about you. You want to make it as easy as possible for your clients to write a review, and many of these sites require that the consumer sign up or log in, which can be a deterrent. Directing them to a review page on your website would be the best option if that feature is available to you.

Timing of Asking for a Testimonial

Be sure to ask for a review when you are fresh on your clients' minds. I don't recommend following up immediately after closing, because, as you can imagine, they are quite busy for a week or so, moving and settling in. Shortly after that (perhaps within 7-10 days), you should send them a link and ask for a review.

If your client is hesitant, because they don't like having to "sign up" on a website to leave a review, ask them to send their thoughts to you in an email. Then, you can use this collateral material in your marketing in other ways to boost your online reputation.

Every Day Action Item:

> If you have past clients, reach out *today*. Ask if they know anyone you can help. If they don't, ask for a testimonial about your character and work ethic. If you don't have any past clients, ask mentors, family and friends to make statements that you could use to get your marketing started.

Chapter Nineteen: Continuous Learning – Stay Current, Stay Relevant

If there is a common thread that I see running from one successful real estate agent to the next, it's the desire to consistently learn and grow. Real estate is an ever-changing industry. Between market trends, the political environment, the economy, technology and global conditions, it can be very difficult to keep up! Keeping yourself exposed to information and being open to change and growth are key to success in any business. In addition to global changes, you also need to keep your finger on the pulse of what's going on in your *local* area.

Here are some things I suggest you use to stay current:

Social Media

You might be thinking, "What? Is she crazy? Social media isn't real!" And, in many cases, I agree. Social media can be a time robber, and there is a lot of garbage to sift through. However, you will hear a lot of "scuttlebutt" (rumors or gossip) on social media that you may have missed otherwise. Your colleagues will often share local events, and it can boost your visibility when you share and attend these events.

Also, on social media you might see news about new businesses opening or a big road construction project that you wouldn't see in traditional media, and you may not hear about unless you know people in the right circles. As an industry professional, these are things that you should be aware of.

Unfortunately, in this day and age, Facebook is one of your best sources for quick access to information. Just be sure to scroll by all the nonsense, and check your facts, before sharing the information.

Groups

There are some good groups related to real estate on Facebook. If you become a member of these groups, you will need to filter out the noise and focus on what's useful. People can be really negative online, and I've seen comments in some groups that made me cringe – but I have also learned from these groups. There may be a discussion on how to handle an impatient or angry seller, and when you weed through the comments, you come away with a few ideas you hadn't thought of before.

There are many real estate professionals out there, who are going through the same things you are. It's nice to have someone to ask for input and advice. Be very careful not to follow any advice that could have legal or ethical implications. Always consult your broker.

Local Classes

There are tons of educational opportunities offered by your local board and local affiliate businesses. Do you have an attorney in your area who does contract classes? Is there an insurance agent who presents recent insurance changes at the board on a regular basis? I know you are absolutely inundated with emails, but perhaps it's time to adjust your radar and pay attention to some of these opportunities. Join the local chamber of commerce and find resources to be in-the-know about upcoming retail and commercial development.

Podcasts

You must keep your general sales skills honed. There are tons of great real estate coaches who have podcasts that you can listen to for free! How much time do you spend driving in your car? A ton, right? Use the time wisely by working in some of these podcasts while you drive, at the gym, while walking, or even while doing office work, if you can listen without being distracted.

Books

Since you are reading this book right now, I know that you are open to gaining new material and ideas through book reading. Don't forget that you can utilize audiobooks, and like podcasts, take advantage of listening to books while you are driving, waiting, working out, etc. And, if you prefer a good fictional paperback during your down time – by all means, indulge. I only suggest you work in a good business-related topic every now and then, to stay sharp!

Blogs

Don't have time for a whole book? You can always subscribe to some quality real estate blogs. Google "real estate blogs," read a few, and see what speaks to you.

Once you subscribe, you will get periodic emails. Sometimes it feels like way too many, and often it feels like they are only trying to sell you something. However, in many cases, there is a ton of valuable information in these blog posts, and you don't have to buy additional services if you don't want to.

However you find your information, continuous learning is going to be a key factor in your ultimate success. Be sure to stay in the know, stay fresh and stay relevant!

Conclusion / The Continuation

The book may have come to an end, but your work has just begun!

It has been my pleasure to engage in conversation with you throughout the pages of this book. My purpose has been to shed light on the reality of building a real estate career and offer some tips and strategies for a strong start. Whether you are in the initial research stages, newly licensed or stuck in your existing career, I sincerely hope that you have gained some insight and direction from reading *Every Day Agent*.

The fact that you are reading this book (and have made it this far) means that you are dedicated to making positive changes and taking meaningful action to work hard in the field of real estate, becoming better at doing what you are already doing. For this, I commend you. The big question is *"Now what?"*

Did you have some "A-ha!" moments while reading this book? At any place did you find yourself nodding your head, relating to the words? Did you capture some new ideas and information that you didn't have before? I truly hope that you have, and I hope that you will take this newly discovered information and these resources and apply them to your Every Day business.

There is no magic sauce in this industry. You will not discover success; you have to make it. You must work hard every day and be willing to stretch outside of your comfort zone. You will need to find discipline within yourself to keep working despite distractions, disappointments, fear or failures. You must take action.

You have the power to achieve greatness, and you *can* be the agent that you want to be. You just need to create a plan and work at it every day. Remember the key topics covered in these pages and lock in your mindset to become a dedicated professional. Focus on your business plan and schedule your time efficiently. Remember, you are the CEO of your business, and if you aren't working to fill your pipeline every day, no one else is going to do it for you.

It is up to *you* to put yourself in the path of opportunities. You need to be out there, talking to people who have a real estate need, engaging in income-generating activities and building your pipeline for future business. Master your skills, practice talking points and learn how to overcome objections, and you will earn the trust and loyalty of potential clients.

Creating an exceptional experience for your client requires that you are educated, informed, organized and always looking out for their best interest. Be prepared, have your systems in place and be responsive to their needs, and you will create lasting relationships that lead to happy customers, and ultimately, repeat and referral business.

These learned and practiced techniques will lead to a thriving real estate career that can sustain itself for decades to come. They can lead to the realization of your wildest dreams.

I want to thank you for coming with me on this journey, and I sincerely hope that you implement the ideas you have learned along the way. Please visit the Every Day Agent community and take advantage of the many resources provided there. I look forward to our further communications through the Every Day Agent Blog or in my discussion group.

It is my goal to better understand your needs, so I can continue to provide useful and relevant information. The more we share and learn from each other, the better we will all be. I commend you for striving to be a leader in this industry and wish you the very best as you build and grow your successful career.

Made in the USA
Monee, IL
23 May 2021